Book Cover Portrait

Frederic Edwin Church (1826-1900)
Hooker and Company Journeying through the Wilderness in 1636 from Plymouth to Hartford, 1846
Oil on canvas
40 1/4 x 60 3/16 in. (102.2 x 152.9 cm)
"Wadsworth Atheneum Museum of Art, Hartford, CT. purchase",
Purchased from the artist before 1850, 1850.9

Pictures Inside The Book

Angelica Schuyler Church Portrait
John-Trumbull-xx-Mrs_-John-Barker-Church-Angelica-Schuyler-
Son-Philip-and-Servant-1785-xx-Private-collection
Courtesy Belvidere Trust

The Church doctors framed photographic genealogical montage
Courtesy Archives, Aylmer Heritage Association

SCAPEGOAT—
SCALES OF JUSTICE BURNING

Supreme Court of Canada Manuscript Ruling

CHRIS PORTER

Order this book online at www.trafford.com
or email orders@trafford.com

Most Trafford titles are also available at major online book retailers.

Printed in the United States of America.

ISBN: 978-1-4907-1665-7 (sc)
ISBN: 978-1-4907-1664-0 (e)

Library of Congress Control Number: 2013922678

Because of the dynamic nature of the Internet, any web addresses or links contained in
this book may have changed since publication and may no longer be valid. The views
expressed in this work are solely those of the author and do not necessarily reflect the
views of the publisher, and the publisher hereby disclaims any responsibility for them.

Trafford rev. 07/22/2014

 www.trafford.com

North America & international
toll-free: 1 888 232 4444 (USA & Canada)
fax: 812 355 4082

To my Wife for her endearing support
To my Son and all those who have had my back and
you know who you are!

CONTENTS

PROLOGUE

I hope you will welcome my book

"Scapegoat—Scales of Justice Burning"

Take the journey to understand the use of one's name and its significance both historically and personally.

This book represents the fusion of historicity and what should be natural justice.

This is my attempt to provide an insight into the factual legal arguments and philosophical understanding as to why the decision to use my name was used in this judgment by the legal, insurance and judicial communities.

This book is dedicated to all those who have been wrongfully accused and used as a scapegoat.

"In matters of Style, swim with the current

In matters of Principle, stand like a rock"

Thomas Jefferson

What inspired me to account for a certain member of the Church
family as mentioned below also became an inspiration to display
the phrase by Thomas Jefferson above since he was a friend of
Angelica Schuyler Church. Thomas Jefferson also describes most
eloquently, the feelings of conviction I have with respect to my
own defence of myself and the truth.

Angelica was the sister of Elizabeth Schuyler Hamilton, the wife

Of

Alexander Hamilton

The First United States Secretary of the Treasury and who was also
the aide-de-camp and confident to

General George Washington the First President of the United
States of America.

Angelica Schuyler Church was the wife

Of

John Barker Church

There are many other stories about Angelica which guide historical writers about her involvement with Thomas Jefferson and perhaps they are more important then the facts we know about this historical figure. How she is described in history should be based on facts not rhetoric similarly to the way in which the Supreme Court of Canada account for Chris Porter in their factual reasons for judgment in,

Whiten v. Pilot Insurance Company SCC 27229

The Supreme Court of Canada erroneously found that I had a train of thought that influenced Pilot Insurance Company to unethically, deny the house fire claim advanced by their insured. The Supreme Court of Canada also declared this in its factual reasons for the judgment without any testimony from me. I did not submit evidence about myself to the Trial Court and the Court of Appeal for Ontario. Neither found that I had a train of thought that influenced Pilot Insurance Company to deny the house fire claim. My name was irrelevant until the Supreme Court of Canada made its ruling.

There is testimonial evidence about me from others, stating that it was not my train of thought as described by the Supreme Court of Canada in its findings, however these facts cannot be found in the factual reasons for judgment in the Supreme Court of Canada ruling. There is also testimonial evidence of who denied the fire claim however these facts cannot be found in the factual reasons in the Supreme Court of Canada judgment. Why the revelation in the Supreme Court of Canada judgment about my name?

The Supreme Court of Canada has recorded in it findings, false accounts of me since February 22, 2002, despite having received material from this book several times.

This book is my attempt to clarify my role and provide details of why I believe I was wrongfully named by the Supreme Court of Canada.

I was not on trial and since I was not a manager at Pilot Insurance Company I was not allowed to give evidence for Pilot.

In its wisdom how did the Supreme Court of Canada make an error describing my role and status as a Senior Claims Manager?

They also know it is not just a mistake in title but also a mistake in identity as the reasons for judgment describe me.

The Supreme Court of Canada made an inference rather than a factual finding, that it was my train of thought that influenced Pilot Insurance Company.

Only as a manager could I be responsible for the company and in my role and status at Pilot Insurance Company I was not a decision maker on large loss claims.

The independent adjuster testified that it was not my train of thought and the lawyer for Pilot Insurance Company identified the Vice President as the person who denied the claim of Keith and Daphne Whiten. At the end of my book I provide certified evidence to support these two statements from the Court of Appeal for Ontario.

Why did the Supreme Court of Canada describe me in its factual reasons of the judgment when there was no factual evidence about me from the lower Court Trial or the Court of Appeal for Ontario?

What follows in this book are the facts of the case as described by me and the consequences of the Supreme Court of Canada's description of Chris Porter.

On the cover of this book is a painting about three historical members of my ancestral family one of which painted the portrait and two of which are in the painting. The painting was completed 210 years after the journey to America is described by the artist. Frederic Edwin Church's "Oil on Canvas", was completed in 1846 of an event he called "Hooker and Company Journeying through the Wilderness in 1636 from Plymouth to Hartford." It was purchased from the artist before 1850 by the Wadsworth Atheneum for $1.30. The Wadsworth Atheneum describes the painting stating that, "The work shows the influence of Thomas Cole—Church's teacher thanks to an introduction from Daniel Wadsworth." I want to thank the Wadsworth Atheneum for allowing me to post the portrait of ancestors related to both the artist and myself. Historians have factually confirmed that this journey did take place and that Richard Church and Anne Marsh did travel with Reverend Thomas Hooker to discover Hartford and that this painting is in fact genuine.

PART ONE

NATURAL JUSTICE?

Pilot Insurance Company

Scapegoat

Chris Porter

The Supreme Court of Canada

Punitive Damages

Whiten v. Pilot Insurance Company

SCC 27229

Manuscript Ruling

Chris Porter

CHAPTER ONE

Controlling Corporate Consequences

Alphonse Gabriel 'Al' Capone, 'Scarface' was well known for his ability to control the justice system in the United States while committing business ventures that to most would be outside the law. This period of time in the history of the United States was considered a very dark time. His method of controlling the justice system, by diverting their attention away from corporate decision makers in his organization, allowed him to function and corporately operate as a gangster in Chicago. Clearly if you remove the fear or influence of the justice system, corporate bad behaviour could become a normative in any society including our own here in Canada.

The Supreme Court of Canada had the last say in a famous case in Canada entitled Whiten v. Pilot Insurance Company. This was a case about a fire insurance claim emanating from a house fire in Haliburton, Ontario on January 18, 1994. Quite simplistically, this claim was advanced by Mr. & Mrs. Whiten on the day their home was totally destroyed by fire on the coldest night of that year in 1994. The claim was actually received at Pilot Insurance on January 18, 1994.

The claim was reported to the branch manager of the Pilot Insurance Peterborough office from another Pilot Insurance branch that had initially received the claim from the insurance broker for Mr. & Mrs. Whiten. The Peterborough branch manager had assigned an independent adjuster and an electrical engineer to investigate and adjust the loss. This was all normal practice for how severe fire loss claims were handled in general. The twist in this story is about how a claims examiner ended up being implicated by the Supreme Court of Canada for his role at Pilot Insurance Company.

I was an employee of Pilot Insurance Company who worked at their head office with the title senior claims examiner reporting to a supervisor, a claims manager, the assistant vice president, (AVP) in charger of claims and in this case the executive vice president and secretary in charge of claims(VP). The Supreme Court found that a 'train of thought' emanated from the senior claims manager who's title was later changed to senior claims examiner, how this train of thought influenced how the corporation Pilot Insurance Company responded to this claim advanced by their insured.

In Canada, the Supreme Court of Canada, receive cases on application for decisions that are being challenged by parties to actions before the Court of Appeal. In this case it was on leave from the Court of Appeal for Ontario. This was a civil action that originated in what was called at the time, Ontario Court (General Division) or what is now called the Superior Court of Ontario. This case was tried before a judge and jury. The jury found that Pilot Insurance Company was in breach of its contractual obligation to provide coverage and also in bad faith in its obligation. The jury awarded the Whitens' full compensation to the extent of coverage under the insurance policy as well as punitive damages which were levied against the corporation Pilot Insurance Company. Punitive damages were assessed at $1,000,000.00, the largest award in Canadian history at that time.

The evidence provided to the Court was presented in the form of both oral and written submissions called factums. Both sides of the trial submit summaries of evidence developed through the process called Examinations for Discovery where both oral and material evidence is scrutinized under oath. The evidence from what is developed at the Examinations for Discovery is usually the central evidence that will be presented at trial.

At the completion of the Trial the jury returns a judgment based on the scale of probabilities, weighing out all the evidence and testimony. The finding in this case was in favour of the plaintiff, which included punitive damages in the amount of $1,000,000.00.

Pilot Insurance Company exercised its right to appeal the judgment to the next level which was to the Court of Appeal for Ontario. Again at this level the Court receives both oral and written submissions by both parties called factums however the factum from Pilot Insurance was to provide arguments to the Court of Appeal regarding errors or other elements of the trial which prevented them from having a fair trial. In other words they must point out errors made by the jury in their findings or the Judge who instructed the jury.

In the Court of Appeal which was heard by three Judges with no jury, they ruled that although Pilot Insurance had breached their obligation to their insured it was not of a sufficient breach to reach the damages assessed by the jury and lowered the punitive damages assessed to $100,000.00. The Court of Appeal for Ontario issued their reasons for judgment in a written decision.

Finally, the case reached the Supreme Court of Canada on Appeal by application by both parties which is the subject of this book. The Supreme Court of Canada also received both oral and written submissions called factums and released a judgment in the form of what is called Reasons for Judgment. The Reasons for Judgment state facts which should only pertain to the evidence and testimony presented to the Superior Court and the Court of Appeal.

In paragraphs 7, 102 and 103 of the judgment, the Supreme Court Judge who wrote the decision for the majority, makes his initial findings regarding the role of the Senior Claims Examiner quoting a reporting letter dated February 25, 1994, from the independent adjuster to Pilot Insurance Company. The Supreme Court Judge also in his findings, states that the Senior Claims Examiner was the Senior Claims Manager at Pilot Insurance Company and also a Claims Examiner as mentioned in paragraph (9) and a Senior Claims

Examiner in paragraph (16). The Judge draws this conclusion as a fact because the report is to the attention of the Claims Examiner. His legal opinion is that this is prima facie evidence on its own and that because the name of the Senior Claims Examiner appeared on the report he is able to conclude that the Senior Claims Examiner had a 'train of thought' that was the catalyst in what drove the corporations Pilot Insurance Company and what is now called AVIVA, a multi-billion dollar company to deny the fire claim advanced by their insured with no evidence.

The Supreme Court of Canada Release New Revised Reasons April 10, 2002

By making this unprecedented change to my title the Supreme Court of Canada must have agreed that there was no evidence or submissions from any party identifying me as a Manager or Senior Claims Manager. Therefore the revised judgment reflecting a correction regarding this error was released a second time on April 10, 2002 and paragraphs 7, 102 and 103 were amended to show my correct title. There was no explanation provided as to how I had been misidentified as a Senior Claims Manager by the Supreme Court of Canada as described in the following paragraphs:

"7) The independent adjuster made further investigations during which he determined that although the Whitens' mortgage payments were in arrears', refinancing was being arranged. It appears that Pilot's Senior Claims Examiner, Mr. Chris Porter, was already moving towards the conclusion that the claim should be disputed based on his suspicions of the family's financial problems. In a letter dated February 25, 1994, the independent adjuster wrote to Pilot:

> As outlined in my 2nd report with the physical evidence we have and the fact that the insured was attempting to arrange financing through another source and pay off the existing mortgage, there is little or no

base [sic] to deny this claim. I certainly agree with your train of thought and if we did not have the physical evidence and the information from the insured's solicitor that he was arranging financing for the Whitens, then my recommendations would certainly be opposite to what they are today. Unfortunately we must deal with the facts on hand and proceed with the adjustment accordingly in my opinion. [Emphasis added.]

102) The respondent claims that an insurer is entirely within its rights to thoroughly investigate a claim and exercise caution in evaluating the circumstances. It is not required to accept the initial views of its investigators. It is perfectly entitled to pursue further inquiries. I agree with these points. The problem here is that Pilot embarked on a "train of thought" as early as February 25, 1994 (see para. 7 above) that led to the arson trial, with nothing to go on except the fact that its policy holder had money problems.

103) The "train of thought" mentioned in the letter to Pilot from independent adjuster kept going long after the requirements of due diligence or prudent practice had been exhausted. There is a difference between due diligence and willful tunnel vision. The jury obviously considered this case to be an outrageous example of the latter. In my view, an award of punitive damages (leaving aside the issue of quantum for the moment) was a rational response on the jury's part to the evidence. It was not an inevitable or unavoidable response, but it was a rational response to what the jury had seen and heard. The jury was obviously incensed at the idea that the respondent would get away with paying no more than it ought to have paid after its initial investigation in 1994 (plus costs). It obviously felt that something more was required to demonstrate to Pilot that its bad faith dealing with this loss claim was not a wise or profitable course of action. The award answered a perceived need for retribution, denunciation and deterrence."

"the above quote from the Supreme Court judgment is a replica and not represented as an official version from the judgment"

CHAPTER TWO

<u>Supreme Court of Canada Mandate?</u>

The case before the Supreme Court of Canada was an appeal regarding a judgment from the Court of Appeal for Ontario. Mr. & Mrs. Whiten appealed the Court of Appeal for Ontario ruling which lowered punitive damages assessed against Pilot Insurance Company from ($1 million dollars) to ($1 hundred thousand dollars).

This case had initially gone to trial at the end of 1995 before the Superior Court of Ontario and was tried by Jury. The Supreme Court of Canada was to review the entire case including all the evidence and testimony to decide whether Punitive Damages were warranted and were of a sufficient amount to reflect the gravity of Bad Faith alleged against Pilot Insurance Company.

The Supreme Court of Canada was to decide whether to restore the Superior Court award of ($1 million dollars) or to rule in favour of the Court of Appeal for Ontario award of ($1 hundred thousand dollars), if punitive damages were warranted in this case.

My name had not appeared in the jury findings of the trial court or in the Court of Appeal for Ontario decision. Therefore the reference to my name by the Supreme Court of Canada was an entirely new twist in the case.

No parties to the case had ever made any claim against me and the Whitens' (Plaintiff's) had never seen my name used in reference to any of the communications with their lawyer.

The parties to the case had not asked the Supreme Court of Canada to assess the role of the Senior Claims Examiner and therefore this was an entirely new twist in the judgment, to focus the attention on the person they believed to have been the mastermind at Pilot Insurance Company. The focus on the examiner rather than Pilot Insurance Company was demonstrated when in their ruling they described the actions to have been an aberration of an individual rather than an implication of a systemic problem with the corporation.

The plaintiff's appealed to the Supreme Court of Canada to restore the award of $1,000,000.00 from the Superior Court. The defendant also appealed to the Supreme Court of Canada in the form of a cross-appeal attempting to argue that the Corporation, Pilot Insurance Company did not act in bad faith. Pilot Insurance presented a factum to the Supreme Court which delineated the blame on senior management to infer that lower level employees were to blame including the Senior Claims Examiner. However this was not presented at the lower Court Trial or to the Court of Appeal for Ontario, and was presented in an effort to defuse the blame and to allow Pilot Insurance Company to control the consequences of decisions made exclusively by senior management. Pilot's senior management made the decision to deny the fire claim advanced by their insured on the basis that the cause of the fire was arson and that the arson was deliberately set by their insured for financial profit.

It is important to go back in history to the very beginning of the first trial to understand how the facts, evidence and allegations of the claim ended up before the Supreme Court of Canada. The information provided in this book are described by me based on my knowledge of the claim and what was discovered since the day the Supreme Court of Canada released their judgment to the public on February 22, 2002.

The reader of this book should be aware that there had never been a thought or concern by me that my name would be used by the very people I worked for and trusted. I never thought my name would be ever mentioned in the Supreme Court of Canada because of my role and my understanding of my involvement in the adjustment of the claim. I was kept in the dark by my employer and therefore had no prior knowledge of how my name was being used by others including Pilot's lower court lawyer and the branch manager when giving evidence under oath. I was not aware of how Pilot's Court of Appeal and Supreme Court lawyer was presenting his defence of Pilot Insurance Company to the Supreme Court of Canada by using my name.

I never testified or provided evidence or an affidavit regarding evidence that was presented by Pilot's lawyers. It was not my train of thought to deny the claim and I was caught off guard and felt ambushed by my name appearing in the Supreme Court Judgment since there was no precedent for my name appearing the Trial or Court of Appeal Judgments. Does a citizen of Canada not have a right to know that his or her name is going to appear in a Supreme Court Judgment before it is published to the world?

Two weeks after the claim was reported to Pilot Insurance Company a lawyer from a Toronto based law firm was hired. This occurred after the AVP and the VP of Claims had a meeting with a lawyer at that firm. The lawyer they had a meeting with had recommended his partner, a lawyer who they had not used in the past but one that the lawyer they knew, had been recommending. I was not involved in the hiring and nor did I recommend the lower court lawyer. There was no evidence of my involvement regarding how the lawyer was hired other than an insinuation by the branch manager and the lower court lawyer during examination for discovery of the branch manager who was the only representative for Pilot Insurance Company and the only employee for Pilot Insurance Company who attended the trial of Mr. and Mrs. Whiten. I requested a number of times to be allowed to attend however I was warned by both the VP and AVP of claims to stay away from the court and to not communicate with their lower court lawyer.

Pilot Insurance Company hired a senior lawyer who represented them before both the Court of Appeal for Ontario and the Supreme Court of Canada. This same lawyer would have assisted Pilot in preparing it's factum for the Court of Appeal for Ontario and the Supreme Court of Canada. In Pilot's factum to the Court of Appeal for Ontario, there is no mention of my name. At that time I was still an employee of Pilot Insurance Company, when Pilot prepared its factum which was submitted on February 27, 1998 to the Court of Appeal for Ontario.

However this all changes at a time when I was no longer an employee with Pilot Insurance Company, when Pilot's submits its factum to the Supreme Court of Canada where my name now appears three times. On page 7 paragraph 17 it states; "After consulting Chris Porter, a senior claims examiner at Pilot's head office, the branch manager decided to obtain counsel on March 8 and formally retained a lawyer (whom he had contacted about a week before) on March 10 1994."

On Page 7 paragraph 17 of the factum to the Supreme Court of Canada it goes on to state; "On March 8, the branch manager told the independent adjuster Pilot was continuing its investigation through its "head office, as they normally do". Mr. Porter and his superior, the Vice-President in charge of claims, was copied with all of the material on the file."

Pilot Insurance Company declared in its factum to the Supreme Court of Canada, that I was copied with all the material on the file. Why did it not make this same declaration in its factum to the Court of Appeal for Ontario?

When we examined the two boxes that contained all the Court Trial records, we did not find evidence that the AVP of Claims and I were copied with the February 3rd and 25th, 1994 reporting letters from the independent adjuster. Pilot's factum inferred that I may have received the letters. The letters in question appear to be to my attention but not as copied as described in the factum. Did Pilot make a slipup when using the word, 'copied' in reference to how I received the letters? Why was this inference quoted as a fact by the Supreme Court of Canada in its reasons?

> "the above quotes are from the Supreme Court and Ontario Court of Appeal judgments and are replica and not represented as an official version from the judgments"

On page 9 paragraph 24 of Pilot's factum to the Court of Appeal for Ontario, it describes how the Branch Manager retained counsel on March 8, 1994. It was revealed that this was after Pilot discovered that the insured's husband had made an assignment in bankruptcy in November 1993. The description is from the plaintiff's counsel's read in extracts of the Discovery transcripts.

In Pilot's factum to the Court of Appeal for Ontario on this same page 9 paragraph 24, it declares without naming a claims person that Pilot retained the second adjuster on June 10, 1994. In this paragraph Pilot also indicated that the first independent adjuster was told that Pilot was continuing its investigation and that this investigation was privileged. No authority is mentioned other than the instruction came from the Branch Manager. There was no mention of my name or even a reference to the Senior Claims Manager or the Senior Claims Examiner.

It is important to understand the twist in the evidence as described in Pilot's factum to the Court of Appeal for Ontario and how it changes in Pilot's factum to the Supreme Court of Canada on page 7, paragraph 17. Perhaps the change was made to demonstrate that I was a directing mind at Pilot when in its factum to the Supreme Court of Canada, it aligns me with the most senior executives at Pilot Insurance Company as if I was one of them.

The following is a excerpt from Pilot's factum to the Supreme Court of Canada, page 7, paragraph 17:

"After consulting Chris Porter, a senior claims examiner at Pilot's head office, the branch manager decided to obtain counsel on March 8 and formally retained the lower court lawyer (whom he had contacted about a week before) on March 10, 1994. On March 8, the branch manager told the independent adjuster, Pilot was continuing its investigation through its "head office, as they normally do". Mr. Porter and his superior, the (assistant to the Vice-President in charge of claims), were copied with all of the material on the file. The Assistant Vice President reported to the Vice President, Executive Vice President and Secretary."

The following is a excerpt from Pilot's factum to the Supreme Court of Canada, page 8, paragraph 18:

"On March 16, 1994, the independent adjuster, without informing the Whitens, wrote a letter to their landlord stating that Pilot would no longer pay rent for their alternative accommodations."

On page 9 paragraph 25 in its factum to the Court of Appeal for Ontario, Pilot describes how the independent adjuster wrote a letter on March 16, 1994 to the insured's landlord stating Pilot would not longer pay the rent for alternative accommodations. Pilot did not inform the insured who learned of the decision from the landlord. The Branch Manager testified he did not know why Pilot made the decision or for that matter who at Pilot Insurance Company made the decision.

It should be noted that the branch manager did not answer this question as he was giving testimony at examinations for discovery but was rather a read-in by the lower court lawyer on behalf of the branch manager on November 29, 1995 just before the trial began.

The following is a quote from the Examination for Discovery of the branch manager dated November 29, 1995;

He is being questioned by the lawyers for Mr. & Mrs. Whiten:

Question:
    And so are you aware of who principally was providing instructions to the lower court lawyer is it the senior claims examiner or the AVP or VP of claims or do you know:

Answer:
    I don't know for certain.

Question:
    Okay. Who made the decision to stop paying the rent for where the Whitens were living?

Answer:
    I think that came down from head office.

Question:
    Do you know who specifically?

Answer:
    No.

Question:
    Do you know why the decision was made to stop paying the rent?

Answer:
    Not exactly, no.

    "the above quotes from the evidence before the Supreme Court is a replica and not represented as an official version of the evidence which was certified by the Court of Appeal for Ontario"

Does the Supreme Court of Canada rely solely on factums presented in an appeal where a significant landmark decision is being proclaimed? Would due diligence of all material facts not compel them to look at all the evidence in the boxes they received from the Court of Appeal for Ontario which also contained all of the evidence and Examination for Discovery testimonial evidence and open trial evidence from the Superior Court of Ontario?

For some reason, although we were able to find a testimonial description of the April 11, 1994 letter from the plaintiff's lawyer requesting the reinstatement of additional living expenses in a report from the independent adjuster to the lower Court lawyer dated April 18, 1994; neither were described in the Supreme Court of Canada findings. Perhaps there was something peculiar about the letter from the lawyer and the independent's description of that letter, or maybe it just had to do with the names on the letter?

CHAPTER THREE

Al Capone Methodology

Why did Pilot Insurance Company not indicate who at head office made the decision to stop paying the insured's additional living expenses? The answer came just days before the Lower Court Trial began and long after the Branch Manager testified at Examinations for Discovery.

That would mean Pilot could formulate the answer it wanted to relay to the Court long after the testimony of the Branch Manager. The answer remained vague and ambiguous and yet this is not a problem when this answer is in the record before the Supreme Court of Canada. How could it not be known who denied the additional living expenses for the Whitens one year after the question is asked?

In an April 18, 1994 report to the lower Court lawyer, the independent adjuster reported, "With respect to the additional living expenses, as you are aware, we terminated payment of these expenses on March 16, 1994 and on the Pilot's instruction, they have not been reinstated. The insured's solicitor is asking that we reinstate those benefits immediately."

On this same page paragraph 4 he states:

"I would ask that you reply to this letter on behalf of the Pilot Insurance Company," The following paragraph (5) the independent adjuster states, "As outlined to you on our April 11, 1994 letter."

Who informed the independent adjuster that the lower court lawyer acting for Pilot Insurance Company held this authority and why does he not copy someone at Pilot Insurance Company with his April 11, 1994 letter?

In its ruling the Supreme Court of Canada state that the AVP of Claims and I are copied with all the material and yet this crucial report is not copied to anyone at Pilot Insurance Company? Perhaps it is because I was absent during this time having back surgery at the Toronto Western Hospital.

The Supreme Court of Canada does not account for the April 11, 1994 letter in its reasons for judgment and that it was ignored when received at Pilot Insurance Company. The letter from the independent adjuster expressed a desperate plea from the lawyer for the insured, to have their additional living expense benefits reinstated.

It is hard to understand why the Supreme Court of Canada in it reasons, does not point out an obvious concern for this letter. What is obvious to me is that the letter came at a time when I was off having back surgery and therefore I could not be aligned with the date of the letter.

The following is a excerpt from Pilot's factum to the Supreme Court of Canada, page 11, paragraph 25:

"On June 9, 1994, the lower court lawyer wrote another letter to the branch manager and Mr. Porter, at Pilot, which was copied to the engineer hired to investigate the cause of the fire for Pilot. Pilot conceded this letter evinced an attitude which gave priority to Pilot's interest at the expense of a dispassionate and fair approach to the interests of Mrs. Whiten. Nevertheless, the letter does not indicate that its author and its recipients were involved in a conspiracy to deny the claim regardless of whether there was evidence of arson or not".

In its factum Pilot Insurance Company is telling the Supreme Court of Canada that one of the recipients of the June 9, 1994 letter was Chris Porter. Pilot suggests that the letter may have left the impression that the recipients of the letter, "were involved in a conspiracy to deny the claim regardless of whether there was evidence of arson or not." By pointing this out in its factum to the Supreme Court of Canada Pilot once again uses my name while negating the entailment of the quote. By pointing this out Pilot brought the question to the forefront and may have assisted the Supreme Court of Canada to manuscript a definition of my role as a decision maker who had the train of thought that influenced Pilot Insurance Company to deny the fire claim.

In it factum to the Supreme Court of Canada, Pilot Insurance Company is providing evidence that was not provided to the Trial Court or the Court of Appeal for Ontario. What motivated Pilot Insurance Company to add my name in their factum to the Supreme Court of Canada without my consent and authorization? Perhaps my former employer was not legally required to inform me, however they must have understood the implications and how this could end up harming my reputation.

The Supreme Court of Canada in its findings, assign the implications of how the lawyer was describing the fire claim in the June 9, 1994 letter to Pilot Insurance Company, to me. The lower Court lawyer uses my name in the letter and therefore once again the Supreme Court of Canada found that this was evidence that implicated my involvement. Again, there was no evidence or testimony from me about receiving the letter and what I had to say about its content. There is no indication in the letter why the lower Court lawyer is writing to me. Once again there are no letters from me responding to this letter. The Supreme Court of Canada can only make an inference about my name appearing on the letter, with no explanation from any testimony from me. What is clear is that the June 9th, 1994 letter does not describe me as a Senior Claims Manager. The following is a quote from the amended reasons of the Supreme Court of Canada judgment:

"17 The attitude of the respondent and its counsel is apparent from the lower court lawyer's reporting letter dated June 9, 1994 to Pilot's Chris Porter and (Pilot's Branch Manager), parts of which read as follows:

The bottom line is that we have moved considerably with the upcoming engineer's report towards successfully denying this claim. We still need more evidence, but we moved significantly in the right direction on June 7th.

18 It appears that all three people directing the respondent's behavior were agreed that the "right direction" was to deny the claim despite the lack of any evidence that the fire had been deliberately set, the lawyer continued"

> "the above quote from the Supreme Court judgment is a replica and not represented as an official version from the judgment"

CHAPTER FOUR

Facts of How The Claim Was Received and Handled

The following are the facts of what transpired and how the claim was handled according to my account as I remember the events many years ago as accurately as I can remember. It should be noted my family and I were scrambling to understand why the Supreme Court of Canada condemned my name and reputation irrevocably.

On the morning of January 19, 1994, the Peterborough Branch Manager telephoned me and provided a brief description of the claim being advanced by Mr. & Mrs. Whiten. I then took that information into the office of the A.V.P. of Claims during a meeting he was having with the Claims Manager and Claims Supervisor. Since this was considered a large loss and the A.V.P. of Claims was specifically responsible for the Peterborough Office, it was expected that I could enter the office and report the claim. The AVP of Claims never informed me that he might have already received a fax report and telephone call on the fire claim. (However, why would the fax copy of the initial report dated January 18, 1994, not have been faxed to his attention?)

There was nothing about arson or an absolute cause of the fire reported to the AVP of Claims in my presentation. That supposition was raised by the AVP in relation to something to do with the financial status of the Whitens'. However during that initial meeting there was a discussion about the suspicious cause of the fire and how the claim should be investigated and what the

AVP of Claims thought about the manager of the Peterborough Office appointing the independent adjuster and engineer to investigate the loss without his consultation and authorization. At the end of the meeting the Claims Manager assured me as we were leaving the office of the AVP of Claims that my role would only be as an examiner on the claim and that the A.V.P. of Claims was in charge of the claim. He explained that this was a Senior Managers claim and it was his prerogative how the claim would be handled. Why did his proclamation not come to fruition when Pilot Insurance Company presented its factum to the Supreme Court of Canada who assigned blame and responsibility to lower level employees including the Senior Claims Examiner?

I was a Senior Claims Examiner. Pilot Insurance Company had various departments in its claim department at Head Office and various roles for examiners and Senior Claims Examiners in various departments such at the Property Claims Department, the Bodily Injury Department and the Accident Benefits Department and the roles between the Claims Managers and the examining staff and Senior Claims Examining staff were stratified and strictly separated.

There were four Claims Managers a Senior Auto Supervisor and a Senior Property Supervisor who divided the responsibility for the 19 offices throughout Ontario which were individually managed by local Branch Managers. There was an Assistant Vice President of Claims and also the Executive Vice President of Claims who over saw the entire claims operation and then the President who became involved in claims of this type of a total loss fire claim where the company had exposure to its reinsurers.

On the date the fire claim was advanced the parent company for Pilot Insurance Company was General Accident with the United States head office located in Philadelphia, Pennsylvania. General Accident was also a reinsurer for Pilot Insurance Company. As a parent company with exposure and reinsurer they may have received a report of any large loss similar to the claim being advanced in this case. It should be noted that at the time of the fire claim in question, General Accident, Commercial Union and Norwich Union and others were merging and becoming, at first a company called CGNU, later CGU, and what is today called AVIVA.

Pilot Insurance Company had been initially owned by General Accident of Perth Scotland however it was sold to General Accident its U.S. subsidiary for about $200,000.000.00 because of significant losses, which was an attempt to bolster General Accident in the United States. There had been a previous transaction in 1986 when General Accident of Scotland acquired the Pilot Insurance Company of Ontario, Canada, from Reliance Insurance Company in Philadelphia. AVIVA reports that at the time Pilot Insurance Company was worth about $200,000,000.00, an interesting number. This approximate number ended up in another issue yet to be described regarding the President and CEO of Pilot Insurance Company.

General Accident played a role in the decision to appoint the new President and CEO of Pilot Insurance Company. Much to the surprise of the Vice President of Claims who may have expected the appointment, however they appointed another individual. General Accident of North America was developing through mergers and acquisitions with companies coming together like USF & G, Canadian General Insurance, Commercial Union, Norwich Union and others just to name a few to create one company called CGU, today known as AVIVA.

In 1997 the corporate lawyers for AVIVA reported that it had been instrumental in mergers and acquisitions for Canadian General Insurance U.S.F&G and the Scottish York Group and a year later when General Accident acquired Canadian General Insurance with the then President becoming President of both corporations. Mergers and acquisitions of companies based in the United States, Europe and Canada required the legal expertise of senior Toronto, Bay Street law firms to assist in these mergers like the law firm where the author of this judgment came from before he was appointed a Supreme Court Judge. This firm was actively involved as corporate lawyers with Canadian General that merged with General Accident. The Supreme Court of Canada Judge who wrote the decision in Whiten v. Pilot Insurance Company had been a Senior Lawyer with a law firm that had been assisting in the acquisitions and mergers of insurance companies from Canada, United States and Europe, such as Canadian General, General Accident and U.S.F. &G., to create what was at one time a company called CGU that is now called AVIVA. This Supreme Court of Canada Judge worked for this law firm from 1986 until January 1998, when he was appointed to the Supreme Court of Canada by the then Prime Minister of Canada.

The senior executives of Pilot Insurance Company were probably instrumental in reporting the fire claim and the Statement of Claim that followed, to Pilot's parent company. Further, this Supreme Court of Canada Judge's law firm, may have become aware of an initial Statement of Claim issued by Mr. & Mrs. Whiten May 27, 1994, claiming among other things, punitive damages in the amount of $125,000.00. Punitive damages would be unprotected by insurance premiums. The funding for this aspect of the claim would come from corporate profits. Therefore this Statement of claim could affect the profits of Pilot Insurance Company and therefore General Accident. There could have been other tax consequences and other consequences that might have influenced other company's willingness to merge or be acquired by CGU.

Therefore this January 18, 1994 fire claim might have become a concern for what was transpiring with what would become one of the largest insurance company's in Canada. Mr. & Mrs. Whitens' claim could have had far reaching consequences for anyone connected with the denial of that claim. The punitive damage claim might have also been a possible embarrassment for Pilot Insurance Company. It was therefore important for the executives to have in place a Scapegoat, fall guy, in the event there was any exposure to them or the company. So began what I call the 'Al Capone' method of controlling the consequences of decisions made by the executives at Pilot Insurance Company and General Accident. The timing of Chris Porter going off for back surgery in March 1994 was a perfect time to ensure that protection. This was the first stage and it had to do with two reporting letters from the independent adjuster to Pilot Insurance Company, namely the February 3, & 25, 1994 reports, both of which were utilized later by this aforementioned Judge in his Supreme Court of Canada Ruling.

> "the above quotes regarding mergers and acquisitions came from the Supreme Court of Canada, General Accident, AVIVA, Pilot Insurance and McCarthy Tétrault LLP McCarthy Tétrault Publications and Websites"

The following is a quote from the amended Supreme Court of Canada Ruling

Paragraph 9

"Pilot requested the Insurance Crime Prevention Bureau, a body set up by the insurance industry, to review the analysis of Pilot's investigator. By letter dated February 25, 1994, the Bureau reported that "we wouldn't have a leg to stand on as far as declining the claim". Pilot, having asked for the opinion, then apparently decided that the Bureau's evaluator was not in fact qualified to render an opinion. No one from Pilot testified as to why the claims examiner, and subsequently Pilot's Branch Manager, rejected this advice as well."

> "the above quote from the Supreme Court judgment is a replica and not represented as an official version from the judgment"

Pilot Insurance Company in its factum to the Supreme Court of Canada and in testimony given on their behalf at Examinations for Discovery stated that I played a significant role in my capacity as a senior claims examiner. Clearly the role did not fit the position in question and that is why in the initial published Supreme Court of Canada Judgment, the title of Senior Claims Manager is recorded.

The reports of February 3, & 25, 1994 clearly indicated that the author was reporting to the person who's train of thought it was at Pilot Insurance Company regarding his suspicion of the alleged cause of the fire, namely arson and his suspicion of the reason for the alleged arson, namely the financial benefits of an insurance claim.

If that person had been me and I had that kind of authority to expose both Pilot Insurance Company and General Accident, then the reasons described by the Supreme Court Judge in paragraph 7 of his judgment are correct and there is clearly no reason to doubt the judgment.

However there are a number of statements made by the independent adjuster which draw into question whether he was speaking to me in those reports. In testimony both the Branch Manager and the independent adjuster make it clear that the independent adjuster was speaking to the Branch Manager in those reports.

There is also the question of my actual role and how it was described by others without my knowledge, consent, presence and without the legal protection as a witness in a legal proceeding in all three levels of court. My role was not drawn into question during the initial trial or when the case was appealed by Pilot Insurance Company to the Ontario Court of Appeal.

Only when it reached the Supreme Court of Canada, where the management of Pilot Insurance Company, who may have been on the board of directors of General Accident (CGU) was my name mentioned in Pilot's factum to the Supreme Court of

Canada, where they mention my name three times drawing a link between the fire claim and Pilot Insurance Company. A very skilful presentation which tied me to the Branch Manager, the lower Court lawyer acting for Pilot Insurance Company and the morality of the denial of the fire claim.

It was at this final stage where Pilot in its factum to the Supreme Court of Canada was trying to introduce a **Scapegoat** so that Pilot would not be blamed for the wrong train of thought of a lower level employee. The scapegoat concept would be fulfilled when the Supreme Court of Canada emphasized the name of a person that had never testified or is called as a witness at Examinations for Discovery or Trial, and whose name is not relevant to the lower Trial Court or the Court of Appeal for Ontario. Did Pilot succeed in influencing the Supreme Court of Canada to find blame with their Scapegoat?

Did I devise a method for controlling the outcome of what would eventually become the largest award for punitive damages in Canadian History with total anonymity?

If we examine more closely the reporting letters of February 3, & 25, 1994, from the independent adjuster to Pilot Insurance Company, did the executives at Pilot Insurance Company create their first means of escape by the use of these letters to include the use of my name or were the letters actually to my attention?

The first letter, namely the February 3, 1994 was not on the letterhead of the adjusting firm where the independent adjuster was employed. It is not known when it was received, by whom and where it was received. Going back to the fax report of January 18, 1994, that first notified Pilot Insurance Company from the Peterborough Office, it is clear that the fax information at the top of the page has been blacked out and the person whose hand writing appears on the report is not identified. The Peterborough Office must have faxed the report to someone otherwise how did it end up as evidence in the initial trial? Why were not the names of those responsible for the claim not clearly identified on this report? What is more interesting is the fact that there is no information on the reports to indicate whether I ever identified these documents.

The Lawyer for Chris Porter Writes to The Supreme Court of Canada Requesting an Amendment and Clarification

On March 22, 2002 a lawyer acting for Chris Porter, sent a letter and faxed a copy to the Registrar of the Supreme Court of Canada. He begins by stating:

"I am retained by Christopher Porter, a former employee of Pilot Insurance Company. I am writing to you further to my discussions with a representative of your office respecting concerns my client has over the accuracy of the facts contained in the Supreme Court Judge's reasons for judgment in the above noted matter. (Whiten vs. Pilot Insurance Company and the independent adjuster Court File Number: 27229)

Mr. Porter was involved in the Whiten claim during his tenure with Pilot. However, his involvement was solely in his capacity as a Claims Examine: not as a Claims Manager or decision maker as the Supreme Court Judge described him in his reasons for judgment. I refer you to paragraph 7 of the Supreme Court Judge's reasons where he finds that Chris Porter was a Senior Claims Manager.

Mr. Porter continues to be employed in the insurance industry with another insurance company where he is engaged in claims examination work. The fact that the Supreme Court Judge found him to be a Claims Manager with Pilot and thus one of the three decision makers (paragraph 18 of the judgment) and one of the middle managers of Pilot (paragraph 16 of the Judgment), when in fact Mr. Porter's role was only that of a claim's examiner who made recommendations and did not have any decision making authority, has had and will continue to have a devastating effect upon his career as a claims examiner and his reputation, which up to this point had been unblemished.

A review of the record before the Court confirms that Mr. Porter's role was solely that of an examiner without any decision-making authority. I refer you to the evidence placed before the court on page **104** of the Appellant's Record. There was no evidence before the court to suggest it was otherwise.

I write to request that this matter be reviewed, specifically the references in the record to Mr. Porter, and if the review confirms that Mr. Porter was not a manager, I ask that the facts as stated by the Supreme Court Judge be revised to reflect that Mr. Porter was an examiner without any decision-making authority.

Thank you in advance for your assistance in connection with this matter.

Signed Chris Porter's Lawyer
Cc.   Chris Porter
        Lawyer for the Plaintiff
        Court of Appeal lawyer for Pilot Insurance Company

The Supreme Court of Canada Responds to the Request

"Dear Chris Porter's Lawyer,

RE: Whiten v. Pilot Insurance Company File 27229

This will confirm that I have received your letter of March 22, 2002, concerning the reasons for judgment in the above noted file.

The Court Issued revised reasons for judgment on April 10, 2002, a copy of which is enclosed for your records. You will note that, at paragraph 7 of the

English version of the reasons the title of Chris Porter has been changed to "Senior Claims Examiner."

All legal publishers have been informed that the reasons are revised. The electronic version accessible through links at the Supreme Court of Canada web site has been updated.

Please do not hesitate to contact me if you have any questions about this. Yours truly,

Registrar

Cc. Lawyer for the Plaintiff, Court of Appeal lawyer for Pilot and other parties

The only change the Supreme Court of Canada was willing to make was to the title Senior Claims Manager which they changed to Senior Claims Examiner. No explanation was provided as to why my name was included in the judgment and why with the change in status and role did not have an effect on the judgment. The response from the Supreme Court of Canada simply did not address my concerns about being named and how I was depicted in the judgment. Should the Supreme Court of Canada not have taken in to consideration the humiliation and defamation I would suffer by the use of my name so prominently displayed in the judgment?

Despite the Supreme Court of Canada's statement that my title had been changed from Senior Claims Manager to Senior Claims Examiner, the defamation continues to be published and is accessible to the public through printed publications and through Internet searches since February 22, 2002. The Judgment was made in a manner with utter disregard for me and my reputation.

Clearly both the Trial Court and the Court of Appeal for Ontario censured the actions of those individuals and the corporation who they found to be responsible. By adding my name to the Supreme Court of Canada's ruling even with the change in title, with no explanation, simply gave the false impression that the rulings of the Trial Court and the Court of Appeal of Ontario also applied to me. Ironically when my name had not even been mentioned in those rulings. But who would look back at those rulings to make sure the Supreme Court of Canada was making an accurate account of previous rulings?

Clearly the Supreme Court of Canada should have realized that the publication of the judgment in print and on the Internet would mean that I would suffer and will suffer severe and lasting damage to my personal and professional reputation. I have suffered considerable distress, embarrassment and humiliation and will suffer non-pecuniary and pecuniary damages.

The reference to my name by the Supreme Court of Canada in this ruling has been repeated many times in legal text by the legal community and referenced in many Trials including Branco v American Home Assurance Company, 2013 SKQB 98 (CanLII); A recent decision of the Saskatchewan Queen's Bench awarded $4.5 million in punitive damages to a disabled employee after a 10-year legal battle with two insurance companies.

Had the Supreme Court of Canada been accountable to the public in the same manner as the public, I could have pursued the Supreme Court of Canada and the Justices who wrote and sanctioned the words uses in the reason for judgment both for a claim in a Court of Law for aggravated and punitive damages for libel.

The Justices of the Supreme Court of Canada and the Supreme Court of Canada are not accountable or subject to the same standards every citizen of Canada must adhere to under Law, Common Law, and the Constitution of Canada. They are not even affected by the Prime Minister of Canada or any other part of the Government of Canada or the Provinces and Territories. The Constitution of Canada does not even protect my name even though there are privacy laws such as The Personal Information Protection and Electronic Documents Act

(PIPEDA) enacted by the Government of Canada that should have provided some protection for a citizen of Canada. Unlike the Constitution of the United States where the words, "We the People" protect every individual even from the Supreme Court, the Charter of Rights and Freedoms in Canada only protect the individual insofar as the State allows. There is a major distinction which I will elucidate about in another chapter of this book.

There does not seem to be any accountability for how or why my name or title was used in the findings of the Supreme Court of Canada judgment. In fact the title they erroneously used was not found in any of the factums presented to the Supreme Court of Canada; these words were simply combined without explanation.

The February 25, 1994 report from the independent adjuster is on his letterhead however the document submitted to Court was a bad photocopy not the original. There is no evidence on this document that I acknowledged receiving this report nor is there any evidence of the executives at Pilot Insurance Company receiving and reviewing this report as submitted by the plaintiff's counsel to the Supreme Court of Canada; a report that was key to the findings of the Supreme Court of Canada in their account of me.

It is this report that the Supreme Court Judge relies upon when naming me as a Senior Claims Manager and having the 'train of thought' that compelled Pilot Insurance Company and General Accident to deny this claim. The train of thought entails the thought of my suspicion of the cause of the fire being arson and my suspicion of the reason Mr. & Mrs. Whiten had for causing the fire, namely for financial gain. Was I the mastermind who fooled the executives of Pilot Insurance Company and the board of directors of General Accident and of course the corporate lawyers who were skillfully coordinating mergers and acquisitions to formulate and create the largest insurance company in Canada?

A revelation begins to unfold about the judgment when, while my wife and I were researching the evidence that was in two large boxes at the Court of Appeal for Ontario. These two boxes and their entire contents were in the Supreme Court of Canada and contained the evidence and the factums of all the parties in the Whiten v. Pilot Insurance Company Appeal. Among the evidence we found a testimonial exchange between the lawyer for the plaintiff's and Pilot Insurance Company's first independent adjuster. This is the person who wrote the two February 3rd and 25th 1994 reports to Pilot Insurance Company and what the Supreme Court of Canada relied upon in its judgment to implicate me.

While giving evidence under oath the independent adjuster is asked by the plaintiff's lawyer about the two February 3rd and 25th 1994 reports to Pilot Insurance Company. The plaintiff's lawyer was asking for him to clarify to whom he was referring when he uses the words your 'train of thought' as quoted by the Supreme Court of Canada in its findings. The original independent adjuster clearly states that it was not the, 'train of thought' of Chris Porter and that he was using those words in reference to another individual at Pilot Insurance Company.

The question was asking the independent adjuster about who at Pilot Insurance Company had the train of thought about the cause of the fire being alleged to be arson, and the suspicion of the cause of the reason for the suspicion, being for financial gain. Should this testimony coming from the very independent adjuster who Supreme Court of Canada quote in paragraph 7 in the reasons for Judgment, that inferred a connection of these very words to me, not have been questioned by the Supreme Court of Canada?

There is also the problem with the documents themselves as to their authenticity as evidence and how they were served to be used as evidence by the lawyer for the plaintiff.

I was not allowed to have a voice in the legal process however when I returned from back surgery and after a period of convalescence the claim was given back to me by the AVP of Claims. I was also given a letter by the AVP of Claims dated June 9, 1994 from the lower court lawyer acting for Pilot Insurance Company. I remember being in so much pain that I could not even lift the claim file.

The letter appears to be bringing the person in charge of the claim up to date on the claim. Was the letter sent to me to bring me up to date because of my absence for back surgery? Or was the letter sent to me to convey to anyone who read the letter that I was in charge of the claim and was on a committee to deny the claim? We will never know because I gave no evidence about the letter.

A news television station in Toronto, Ontario Canada called W5 of CTV displays this letter in a show called Risky Business, of course without ever speaking with me and confirming my role and status in the role Pilot Insurance Company, General Accident and the Supreme Court of Canada want to allege.

Therefore the June 9, 1994 letter may have been sent to me in the event the letter was submitted as evidence to reveal the train of thought at Pilot Insurance Company just before the claim was denied. This would add a buffer between the intent of Senior Claims Management and the denial of the claim by Pilot Insurance Company. Interestingly enough, there were no acknowledgement letters from me to either the independent adjuster or the lower Court lawyer acting for Pilot Insurance Company about this letter.

Why would both the independent adjuster and lower court lawyer take such a risk without written authority from Pilot Insurance Company, their employer and sticking their necks out for someone who had never acknowledged or directed anything in writing to either party? Is that the way normal lawyers and independent adjusters respond to directions being given on serious claims? The absence of written directions from Pilot Insurance Company to its retained lawyer and independent adjuster was of no concern for Senior Claims Management on an important claim.

During Examinations for Discovery both the Branch Manager and lower Court lawyer acting for Pilot Insurance Company, it was stated that I played the part of recommending the defence lawyer. That same testimony was repeated in Pilot's factum to the Supreme Court of Canada. However this statement was not used in Pilot's factum to the Court of Appeal for Ontario.

In Pilot's factum to the Supreme Court of Canada it makes the same implication about my role in appointing the lower Court lawyer. This lower Court lawyer implied during Examinations for Discovery that although he was present at the back of the office of the VP of Claims for Pilot Insurance Company when I presented the facts of the fire claim to the VP of Claims. The VP of Claims then made the decision to deny the claim. The lower Court lawyer implied that he did not suggest how the claim should be handled or denied. The only thing in writing that followed this meeting was in the form of Pilot's Statement of Defence.

Pilot Insurance Company had in place a procedure whereby the Peterborough Branch Manager would report to his counterpart in Head Office on serious claims such as the Whiten claim. However, initially he would report by a phone call to me if he could not reach the VP of claims directly. However, the Senior Claims Examiner would not have any authority to provide direction and it would be expected as a matter of procedure that the information would be provided to the VP of Claims by the Senior Claims Examiner. The Senior Claims Examiner did not have the authority to give the Branch Manager direction on how the claim would be handled but could relay back to him the comments of the VP of Claim if they were not significant. Clearly the implication of an arson allegation would not be accepted by the Branch Manager from the Senior Claims Examiner and nor was this within his authority. In this case it was not the opinion of the Branch Manager or the Senior Claims Examiner that the allegation of arson was warranted in the initial report.

My role as the Senior Claims Examiner was described by the lower Court lawyer and Branch Manager as insignificant when it came to having authority at Pilot Insurance Company. If the words lowly employee were used by the lower Court lawyer and Branch Manager to describe me at Examinations for Discovery, then how did an employee in such a position lead the company into disaster without being noticed? Again to be consistent how does a lowly employee appoint defence counsel, instruct defence strategy, receive letters such as the June 9, 1994, and be on a committee with Executives to provide authoritative direction in the denial of a significant fire claim?

The lower Court lawyer acting for Pilot Insurance Company declared to the Court that his relationship with me was privileged. He and Pilot Insurance Company needed one person who would not be called to give evidence. So Pilot Insurance Company and the lower Court lawyer picked the one person who had no authority or involvement in the decision making process. Pilot Insurance Company had the lower Court lawyer provide me with an envelope, which I was to never open, entitled 'For Your Eyes Only'.

528.	R	MR. MSI: Okay, fair enough. I gather for the same reasons that you gave in respect of Mr. Porter's file, and I am going to ask for your entire fire, Mr. Crabbe. I take it you're refusing?
		MR. CRABBE: And you're serious?
529.		MR. MSI: Yes.
		MR. CRABBE: Well, I'm serious about my answer that you're not going to get it.

"The above quote is from the Court of Appeal for Ontario and is a replica and not represented as an official version from Examinations for Discovery"

The receipt of this envelope from the AVP of Claims, seemed to supported my understanding, that as far as I was concerned the lower Court lawyer and I were in a solicitor client protected status. Since solicitor client privilege was declared and I might add at the displeasure of the plaintiff's representatives, why was any evidence relating to me presented by Pilot Insurance Company in Court?

Evidence from the Branch Manager and the lower Court lawyer about the role of the Senior Claims Examiner at Examination for Discovery was presented at the same time the lower Court lawyer was declaring solicitor client privilege regarding that same evidence about me. Perhaps the only privilege was that I was unaware of knowing what was being said about me and questions being asked about me by the representatives for the plaintiff. Clearly anyone would want to know that evidence such as the February 3rd and 25th 1994 reporting letters, where their name was being used, was being described by the very person who declared that my evidence was privileged.

Since the relationship between the Senior Claims Examiner and the lower Court lawyer was declared privileged by the lower Court lawyer, would one not wonder why evidence was being provided to the Court of such importance where the Senior Claims Examiner's name appears in such a conspicuous manner and was being done in his absence? The letters in question that we found in the record in the two boxes at the Court of Appeal for Ontario did not appear to come from the Head Office file because there was nothing identifying them such as a stamp or signature and they were clearly not originals. So why when the reporting letters were so important, was I kept from testifying about them and why did Pilot Insurance Company describe my involvement with the letters when the Branch Manager and lower Court lawyer gave evidence about them and used my name in reference to them?

I had requested to attend trial and therefore would not have proposed that I be subjected to solicitor client privilege. However I did not have authority to change these conditions. It was explained to me that I could not testify, the plaintiff's could not call me to testify, and no evidence could be presented about me that implicate me in any way shape or form. I was told by Pilot Insurance Company Claims Management and its Counsel that this solicitor client privilege existed indefinitely and I assumed up to the point when Pilot Insurance Company presented its factum to the Supreme Court of Canada.

The Supreme Court of Canada Judgment in Whiten v. Pilot Insurance Company SCC 27229, was released on February 22, 2002 along with the words that the train of thought to deny the insurance claim was fostered by the Senior Claims Manger, Chris Porter. Although the word Rogue was used in reference to the claim file it also implicated the handler which was me, as inferred by the Supreme Court of Canada in its findings.

The Supreme Court of Canada also assigned the word delinquent to the handler's of the claim file who should move on to another line of work, again implicating me. Finally, the Supreme Court of Canada found that my attitude influenced the hiring of the second adjuster and engineer and that I was on a committee to deny the claim. That I also prolonged the denial of the claim for an indefinite period of time well beyond reasonable prudence to force the insured to either abandon their claim or take a lowball settlement.

This was a landmark ruling by the Supreme Court of Canada, published in hardcopy and by many Internet sites that publish Supreme Court of Canada judgments. The ruling was received, not just here in Canada, but around the world because of the subject matter. The Supreme Court of Canada has indicated that this ruling is one of the most referenced cases in Canadian history.

The behavior of the Senior Claims Manager, as described by the Supreme Court of Canada, was allowed to transpire even with the executives of Pilot Insurance Company receiving copies of the reporting materials. It is all Chris Porter if you believe the

Supreme Court of Canada; someone who could not have an affect on the Corporation and who was of no significance, certainly not a fiduciary.

I guess it would take a genius to figure that out and perhaps that is why Pilot Insurance Company and General Accident were so content to close the book on this subject. Sounds like an Al Capone resolution rather than real justice. Is it possible I had an opposite role and position with respect to how the claim should have been handled from the beginning? My role was to provide the AVP of claims with all reports received at head office from the Peterborough branch and to inform him of anything that developed from other entities including any reports that inadvertently came to me from the lower court lawyer. My involvement in the case ended on the Friday before the lower court trial began and I was told to have nothing to do with the trial lawyer and to not receive any communications from him. At times when he did call me I brought the AVP of Claims to my desk to respond directly to the lawyer. I wasn't just asked not to communicate with the trial lawyer but warned not to have any discussion with him.

A lawyer with an AVIVA law firm published a book regarding Good Faith and Insurance Law by Canada Law Books and quotes the Supreme Court reasons in Whiten v. Pilot Insurance Company as an example of a Bad Faith claim. He uses the 'train of thought' quote and the February 25, 1994 letter from the independent adjuster to Pilot Insurance Company to exemplify my role at Pilot Insurance Company (without specifically naming him). Of course he does not even speak with me about the accuracy of the Supreme Court ruling and even after receiving evidence that contradicts the conclusion reached by the Supreme Court, continues to promote the book without explaining to the public my role as demonstrated by the evidence he was provided. That was the same attitude I received when I complained to a law firm in Quebec, lawyers for Pilot Insurance Company and General Accident who published an article about the judgment using my name and declaring to over 450 insurance companies around the world and on their website live on the Internet, that I was the Senior Claims Manager who denied the claim for Mr. & Mrs. Whiten. This ended my insurance career.

I sued this Quebec law firm for libel and the lawsuit began in 2003 and was fought for three years until this senior Quebec law firm finally conceded that I was not the person who denied the claim and was not a Senior Claims Manager. The issue of the Claims Manager title is significant even though it was not the significant complaint raised by the lawyer representing me with the Supreme Court of Canada in February 2002 after the ruling was released. The issues raised in my lawyer's communication with the Supreme Court of Canada emphasized more about my role being misunderstood than the importance of identifying me as a Senior Claims Manager in their ruling.

In the response letter from the Registrar of the Supreme Court of Canada they did not provide any explanation as to why they used the title in the first place. They did not receive this information in the factums presented in the Supreme Court of Canada and it was not in evidence or in any of the factums in the lower Court Trial or in the Court of Appeal for Ontario.

However even changing the title to senior claims examiner did not create a question as to how I could have masterminded this event from a position that was beneath the status and role of a manager or executive at Pilot Insurance Company and General Accident. It certainly does not explain how I was described as both a Senior Claims Manager and Examiner in the same judgment. However once this error had to be corrected, the false account of my role and status was once again re-established in the libelous article by the Quebec law firm and sent to 450 insurance companies by hard copy and around the world on the Internet from the law firm's website.

This law firm also acted for General Accident currently known as AVIVA and was acting with their authority having provided a hardcopy to their executives on the falsity of the allegations they were making in their libelous publication about me. It was not done in a closet. Perhaps AVIVA wanted the public to be aware that I was the directing mind at Pilot Insurance Company. Perhaps that is why the Quebec law firm was required by another AVIVA law firm to repost the libelous statement on the Internet a second time after the Quebec law firm initially removed it from the Internet. The AVIVA law firm appointed to defend the Quebec law firm were acting under the directions of AVIVA (Pilot Insurance Company) and had advised the Quebec law firm to put the libelous article about me, back on their law firm's website and therefore the Internet a second time. The AVIVA appointed lawyer acting to defend the Quebec law firm in the libel action directed the Quebec law firm to repost the libelous article. I therefore sued the Quebec law firm a second time and had two actions before the Superior Court of Ontario.

Even before Examinations for Discovery were held the Superior Court of Ontario in a motion dismissed both actions and reduced the legal defence costs I would have to pay the Quebec law firm to $56,000.00 which was later reduced to $25,000.00. The case was well described in the Ontario Reports by a former editor of the Ontario Reports who is currently with the Superior Court of Ontario. This remained the case until it reached the Court of Appeal for Ontario which unanimously re-established both actions to be tried on the basis that I was entitled to a trial on the matter of libel and that the argument for Qualified Privilege had not been established by the Quebec Law firm and their lawyer. This second decision was buried in the legal community and yet the first ruling is easily accessible without reference to the case being overturned by the Court of Appeal.

Only one law firm in all of Canada in Vancouver by the name of McConchie Law, have published and acknowledged the outcome of the litigation of this matter. The two lawsuits finally reached trial before the Superior Court of Ontario who heard the case for three days during which the trial judge allowed me to speak openly about who was actually responsible for the denial of the claim for Mr. & Mrs. Whiten and to describe my actual role at Pilot Insurance Company. The cases were settled with an apology letter being given to me by the Quebec law firm on condition that it not be published or put on the Internet. They also agreed to remove the libelous article from their website which was the most important achievement for me because I felt the absence of such an article would allow me to once again work in the insurance industry as a claims examiner.

However, the libelous publication along with the Supreme Court ruling had caused irreversible damage to me and my reputation and my ability to earn a living.

Since February 22, 2002 I have tried to have the Supreme Court of Canada explain why my name was mentioned in their ruling. I was not accused by Mr. & Mrs. Whiten, Pilot Insurance Company or General Accident? No claim was ever brought against me and no subpoena was ever issued or served on me to testify.

In fact when my family and I visited Mrs. Whiten after the death of her husband a few years prior, she and her son displayed all the letters they had compiled from Pilot Insurance Company and their lawyer and could not find one reference to my name. Again could you imagine how I masterminded this entire event and remained so anonymous? So why it was so important for the Supreme Court of Canada to use my name so prominently displayed in such a landmark Judgment when the person is not a party to the proceedings? I was not a party to the case and as declared to the Trial Court, not even a potential witness. My status was in the record, in the boxes of evidence at the Court of Appeal for Ontario. The Court of Appeal for Ontario identified these boxes and certified that they had been sent to the Supreme Court of Canada.

Why did the Supreme Court of Canada find that in such a landmark decision it was necessary to expose an otherwise private and innocent citizen of Canada and lowly employee of Pilot Insurance Company to such widespread ridicule and condemnation? The Supreme Court of Canada had the declaration of privilege as evidence in its record. It was therefore evident that their findings as they described me were condemning a person who unwittingly was not able to testify in the past and therefore did not even have a voice in the decision making process.

In its ruling the Supreme Court of Canada was unanimous, except for one justice; however my name remained prominently displayed with factual inaccuracies to do with my title and role in the condemnation by the Court. Perhaps they felt I was a deserving mastermind of the worst case of bad faith in Canadian history. The Supreme Court of Canada has not explained adequately, why the information provided by me and my lawyer was insufficient to make any changes to the judgment to include the removal of my name. Or at least provide an amendment to accurately explain to the public my role if my name was to continue to be referenced in the factual reasons for judgment.

I have hired three lawyers, had complaints with the Canadian Judicial Council that were reviewed twice, corresponded with Prime Ministers, Ministers of Justices, Attorney Generals, both Provincially and Nationally, The Human Rights Commission, Justice Department, and every department associated with justice in Canada and not one department or entity has provided any assistance. Pilot Insurance Company and General Accident have shown nothing but distain towards their former employee.

On November 11, 2002 the Supreme Court of Canada ruling finally short circuited and ended my insurance career while I was an employee with another insurance company. While I was in direct discussions with the Supreme Court of Canada and with the then Minister of Justice, my claims manager decided I should handle a claim for them wherein a claim for bad faith had been alleged.

The insured in this case was having his claim denied by my employer. After reviewing the material of the claim file, which had previously been handled by another adjuster for over a year, I was concerned about the merits of the denial of coverage. A partner of the law firm that represented the insured was a well known coverage expert and I had worked with this lawyer for a number of years, including while I was employed with Pilot Insurance Company. I contacted this lawyer off the record and discuss the merits of our case in general terms. I was concerned about the merits of the denial of coverage in this case and also my personal involvement because of the Supreme Court of Canada decision, where my name was mentioned in Whiten v. Pilot Insurance Company. This lawyer advised against my involvement in the claim in question because of the Supreme Court of Canada ruling; concerned because this might have given greater exposure to my company with me on the case.

After reviewing the case and in light of what I had been advised, informed my employer that they would not have a leg to stand on and to pay the claim. Instead of taking my advice my manager sent a formal complaint to the VP of Claims requiring that I accept the charge that I had refused to accept an assignment.

It was not known at the time that my employer had already received the libelous communiqué from the Senior Quebec Law firm and that this letter and the Supreme Court of Canada decision were determining the outcome of my employment as a Claims Adjuster.

On the day I was dismissed, I was returning from visiting the grave of my great-grandfather with my parents on November 11, 2002. Prior to my demise my lawyer sent a letter to a lawyer appointed by Pilot Insurance Company. I had previously approached this same libel lawyer shortly after the Supreme Court of Canada Ruling in Whiten v. Pilot Insurance Company and he advised me at the time that he did not believe I had any concerns about the reference to my name in the Judgment with either the Supreme Court of Canada or Pilot Insurance Company.

I was seeking advice from him for the purposes of representing my interests. It turned out that he was actually employed by Pilot Insurance Company to respond to any issues I would have with them over this ruling. My lawyer therefore wrote a letter on my behalf to this lawyer acting for Pilot Insurance Company; however this same lawyer advised that Pilot Insurance Company would be unwilling to provide any assistance that would have allow me to continue to work as a claims examiner.

The following is a summary of a letter my lawyer sent to the President of Pilot Insurance Company via to the lawyer representing Pilot Insurance Company. The request was made well before I was dismissed and could have helped prevent what was about to happen with my employer.

There is no doubt that the President of Pilot Insurance along with the VP of claims were attempting to deflect criticism of management's handling of this claim to lower level claims employees including me. This was clearly a breach of Pilot Insurance Company's obligation as an employer to its current and former employees.

The executives of Pilot Insurance Company were made aware of my lawyer's March 22, 2002 correspondence with the Supreme Court of Canada and that the Registrar had responded affirmatively with changes to my title. As described in evidence at the end of chapter 11, there is no doubt that a decision to deny the Whiten fire claim and retain counsel with instructions to put forth a vigorous defence was ultimately made by the VP of Claims.

Correspondence from my counsel to the Registrar of the Supreme Court of Canada was provided to Pilot Insurance Company and their counsel and they were aware that he had been requesting that the Judge's findings be amended so as to reflect the fact that I was an examiner without any decision-making authority. Despite the request of counsel for Pilot Insurance Company and the executives of Pilot Insurance to correspond with the Supreme Court of Canada to state, that I not only had no decision-making authority at Pilot Insurance Company to settle this claim but had in fact recommended to the Assistant Vice President and the Executive Vice President of Claim's prior to the case going to trial that the claim be paid, Pilot took no steps whatsoever to absolve me of any involvement in the decision to deny the Whitens claim.

Pilot Insurance Company's executives were well aware that I continued to earn my livelihood as a claims examiner in the insurance industry and would therefore be directly affected by the Supreme Court ruling. Pilot was also aware that by fostering the perception that I made the decision to deny the Whiten claim it would cause serious damage to my reputation in the insurance industry. Therefore the President of Pilot Insurance Company was well aware of the damage he would cause me in his statement as reported in Thompson's World Insurance News on March 1, 2002 that "Where we made our errors was in not monitoring this as it went through the various steps." This statement was clearly blaming lower level employees for how the claim was handled which was the opposite of what happened.

In the letter my lawyer wrote to Pilot Insurance Company, he was chastising them for not stepping in to help me as my former employer. He pointed out that if Pilot's counsel had written a letter to the Supreme Court of Canada, shortly after the ruling was released to the public on February 22, 2002, stating Pilot had reviewed the Whiten decision and wished to correct any misunderstandings as to who made the decision to deny the claim and pursue the arson defence. That this letter could have had an effect on the Court's willingness to correct their account of my involvement in the decision to deny the fire claim. By not corresponding with the Supreme Court of Canada, on my behalf, Pilot Insurance Company gave the impression that they were satisfied with the mistaken belief that I was one of the decision makers and caused irreparable damaged to my reputation in the insurance industry.

CHAPTER FIVE

Assumptions Regarding Use of My Name

In its findings, the Supreme Court of Canada found that there was sufficient factual evidence about me when my name appears in the first two reporting letters and the June 9th, 1994 letter, to make an inference about my name, title and role as well as my train of thought in the ruling under what is entitled in the judgment factual reasons.

The letters were not given in evidence from my file but may have come from the independent adjuster's file and the lower Court lawyer's file. My file had been declared privileged by the lower Court lawyer so they did not come from my file.

What remains puzzling is why my file and my testimony was declared privileged and at the same time the file belonging to the original independent adjuster was taken by Pilot's lower Court lawyer soon after he was retained in 1994.

Did someone at Pilot Insurance Company tell the lower Court lawyer to take the original independent adjuster's file? The file was not returned by the lower Court lawyer to the independent adjuster, until the lawyer was ordered to by the Trial Judge when the independent adjuster was testifying during the Trial. It was also given back to him disassembled.

The independent adjuster, testified that the file contained copies of the first two reporting letters and may have also contained other correspondence between himself, Pilot Insurance Company and the lower Court lawyer as well as the expert witnesses and possibly the plaintiff counsel's letters. The file would have also reflected the fact that there were no letters from me. Clearly comparing the previously unblemished independent adjuster's file with what it contained to the head office file might have given some semblance of credibility to the three aforementioned reporting letters which were relied upon by the Supreme Court of Canada.

Letters introduced at trial where my name appeared were allegedly photocopies and not from my file. However there was evidence in the trial record pages 589, 594, 595 & 596 in Volume (I) one, as to who was receiving the information from those letters and to whom the independent adjuster was speaking. The Court of Appeal for Ontario has certified a document that reveals that these documents had been sent to the Supreme Court of Canada however because the document is dated December 18, 1998 it is unclear when the Court of Appeal for Ontario sent the material. Was it sent to the Supreme Court before applications were presented for an appeal either by the plaintiff or the defendant?

The Supreme Court concluded that there were letters talking to me and that bad photocopies of those letters were genuine, without testimony or an affidavit from me.

The Supreme Court Judge stated in paragraph seven (7) of his reasons that a paragraph in one of the reporting letters from the independent adjuster to Pilot Insurance Company, demonstrated my train of thought and therefore the train of thought of Pilot Insurance Company. The only page throughout the entire trial transcript where the train of thought is clearly described is on pages 595 and 596. The independent adjuster testified that it was not my train of thought about the suspicion of the fire or the concern for the Whitens finances. He assigns that train of thought to an individual who had authority at Pilot Insurance Company, an individual who testified on behalf of Pilot Insurance Company.

The Court of Appeal for Ontario describes evidence before them in their reasons in C23973 paragraph (12) "Because of the Whitens' precarious financial situation and because he suspected arson, Pilot's claims manager asked the Insurance Crime Prevention Bureau".

The Supreme Court of Canada describes this same evidence before them in the Judge's reasons SCC 27229 paragraph (fact) (9) "Pilot requested the Insurance Crime Prevention Bureau". Obviously, he leaves out the words claims manager. The Court of Appeal for Ontario describes evidence before them in this same paragraph stating the following; "No one from Pilot testified why the claims manager took this position".

The Supreme Court Judge, with the same evidence states in paragraph (9), "No one from Pilot testified as to why the claims examiner, and subsequently Pilot's Branch Manager, rejected this advice as well".

In paragraph (7) the Supreme Court Judge describes me as a Senior Claims Manager, in the first publication of the reasons, therefore who was the claims examiner in paragraph (9)? Why did he add this person to the statement made by the Court of Appeal? Clearly on page 594 of the Trial Record it demonstrates as described in testimony from the independent adjuster who held this opinion of the Insurance Crime Prevention Bureau's conclusions as to their opinion on whether the cause of the fire was arson. It was clearly not me as described by the Supreme Court Judge.

> "the above quotes are from the Supreme Court and Ontario Court of Appeal judgments and are replica and not represented as an official version from the judgments"

In further testimony from the independent adjuster, while being questioned by counsel for Keith and Daphne Whiten, on page 589 of the trial transcript, in referring to the February 25, 1994 reporting letter from the independent adjuster to Pilot Insurance he qualifies who he is speaking to at Pilot in his report of February 3, 1994. He qualifies that it is not me. This along with other testimony as quoted above, that although the poor photocopy of the February 25, 1994 letter contains my name, it is clear that the independent adjuster is not addressing me. He established whom he is addressing when testifying at the trial.

The Supreme Court clearly makes a change from the decisions of the Court of Appeal for Ontario and the Superior Court of Ontario. Although the other two courts condemn Pilot Insurance Company and rule in favor of a punitive damage award for bad faith, the Supreme Court clearly want to condemn the author of the bad faith. In the Supreme Court Judge's reasons this is clearly demonstrated in paragraphs 7, 8, 9, 16, 17, 18, 102, 103, 104, 130, 160 and 162.

Why did the Supreme Court of Canada not quote page 1348 in volume two of the Trial record in its factual reasons for judgment? The Court of Appeal for Ontario have certified a copy of this evidence and also certified a document indicating that the Supreme Court of Canada had the evidence from Examinations for Discovery of Pilot Insurance Company, as to who denied the fire claim. The Supreme Court of Canada would not have been making an inference when naming this person and they would not have made an error about his title, train of thought and his role at Pilot Insurance Company in the adjustment of the insured's fire claim.

In my libel lawsuit with the Senior Quebec Law firm, the lawsuit was over a similar incorrect description of my role in Whiten v. Pilot Insurance Company. This as described in testimony from the law firm was the result of the Supreme Court of Canada's reasons in the Supreme Court decision. It is clear that neither reviewed key evidence in the trial record and this record was in the Supreme Court until well after both publications were being created and printed.

The President of Pilot Insurance Company
Charged and Convicted by
The Financial Services Commission of Ontario
(FSCO)

This case involved a false report by the President of Pilot Insurance Company to FSCO in the amount of almost two hundred million dollars. The amount of money in question was over a reserve issue at the same time the Whiten decision was being rendered in 2002. In other words FSCO are saying that the President of Pilot Insurance Company deceived them in his reporting the finances of Pilot Insurance Company. In order for the executives to use my name in place of their own it would have required the authority of the President and CEO of Pilot Insurance Company. It was this President who spoke out in the media just after the Supreme Court of Canada returned the judgment, blaming lower level employees for the Whiten case, clearly pointing his finger at me.

When the ruling was released, very early on, my lawyer tried to convince Pilot Insurance Company to attempt to have the Supreme Court of Canada amended their judgment, however they refused. Was the reaction and announcement made by the President of Pilot Insurance Company an indication that I was being used as their **scapegoat?**

CHAPTER SIX

<u>Misidentifying My Role</u>

The Supreme Court of Canada ruling misidentified my role in paragraphs 19 and 130 in the reasons as follows:

19) "The reference to the two "previous fires" was firstly to a fire that occurred in a cottage owned by the Whitens' son-in-law but rented out to a (T) and secondly to another fire in another house previously occupied by (T). There was no apparent connection to the appellant or her family. At the Court of Appeal, Pilot conceded that evidence about these two fires was irrelevant and inadmissible. The reporting letter of June 9th continues:"

130) "The respondent points out that there is no evidence this case represents a deliberate corporate strategy as opposed to an isolated, mishandled file that ran amok. This is true, but it is also true that Pilot declined to call evidence to explain why this file ran amok, and what steps, if any, have been taken to prevent a recurrence."

> "the above quote from the Supreme Court judgment is a replica and not represented as an official version from the judgment the letter T is used in place of the real name"

No deliberate corporate strategy at a time when every executive at Pilot Insurance Company were subject to the pitfalls of merging with General Accident. Why would former employees even at the executive level at Pilot Insurance Company be concerned with a loss ratio when their success and job security is being watched by the very people who oversaw this claim from beginning to the end? Perhaps that is consistent with the findings of FSCO, The Financial Services Commission of Ontario when they charged the same executive President and CEO of Pilot Insurance Company and possibly a member of the Board of Directors at General Accident (CGU). The following is the announcement on the FSCO website of their ruling that pertained to an almost two hundred million dollar reserve shortfall in the President's reporting of the finances of Pilot Insurance Company in the year Supreme Court of Canada judgment came down in Whiten v. Pilot Insurance Company.

It was after the release of the Supreme Court of Canada ruling of Whiten v. Pilot Insurance Company that the President announced overwhelming profits for Pilot Insurance Company. Why was there not widespread reporting of the FSCO decision and the credibility of the inference this same President made in his statement to the media, of how upper management were not monitoring lower staff including the Senior Claims Examiner as decisions were being made on what turned out at that time to be the largest punitive damages claim in Canadian History?

The following is copied from the FSCO website which only provides limited information into the judgment, reasons for judgment in the case involving the then, President and CEO of Pilot Insurance Company, and surprisingly enough the person who had the last say in how Pilot Insurance Company was going to handle the claim for Mr. & Mrs. Whiten and the exposure Chris Porter was going to be subjected to by allowing the introduction his name into the Supreme Court of Canada where Pilot's counsel misrepresented him as a decision maker at Pilot Insurance Company and the person who influenced what would become the largest punitive damage claim awarded in Canadian History.

Cease and Desist Order Against The President of Pilot Insurance Company

Credit FISCO@: @ Queen's Printer for Ontario. The following information is a replica excluding the actual name of the President from the FISCO report.

SUPERINTENDENT OF FINANCIAL SERVICES

REGARDING the Insurance Act, R.S.O. 1990, c. I. 8, as amended, (the "Act") in particular sections 441 and 447

AND REGARDING The President of Pilot Insurance Company

CEASE AND DESIST ORDER

The Superintendent of Financial Services ("Superintendent") is of the opinion that the President of Pilot Insurance Company committed an unfair or deceptive act or practice by furnishing misleading or incomplete information to the Financial Services Commission of Ontario. The particulars are set out in Schedule "A" attached to, and forming part of, this Order.

The President of Pilot Insurance Company chooses not to contest the proposed order and waives the procedural requirement under section 441(2) of the Act for a Notice of Intention to make an order and his right under section 441(3) to request a hearing.

TAKE NOTICE THAT pursuant to section 441(7) of the Act, AND WITH THE CONSENT OF The President of Pilot Insurance, the Superintendent hereby orders that The President of Pilot Insurance Company cease and desist from, directly or indirectly, engaging in the business of insurance or carrying on the business of insurance, or otherwise undertaking insurance on behalf of another person or as an insurer, an agent or an adjuster or an employee or representative of an insurer or an agent or an adjuster, for a period of two (2) years from the date of the Cease and Desist Order.

AND TAKE NOTICE THAT section 447(2)(b) of the Act provides that any person who fails to comply with any order made under the Act is guilty of an offence and liable on a first conviction to a fine of not more than $100,000 and on each subsequent conviction to a fine of not more than $200,000.

AND FURTHER TAKE NOTICE THAT section 447(4) of the Act provides that every director, officer and chief agent of a corporation who caused, authorized, permitted or participated in a corporation committing an offence, or who fails to take reasonable care to prevent a corporation from committing an offence, is also guilty of an offence and is liable on a first conviction to a fine of not more than $100,000 and on each subsequent conviction to a fine of not more than $200,000.

ISSUED AT the City of Toronto this 31st day of January, 2007

Chief Executive Officer and
Superintendent of Financial Services

CHRIS PORTER

SUPERINTENDENT OF FINANCIAL SERVICES

CEASE AND DESIST ORDER

The Superintendent of Financial Services ("Superintendent") is of the opinion that Kistruck committed an unfair or deceptive act or practice by furnishing misleading or incomplete information to the Financial Services Commission of Ontario. The particulars are set out in Schedule "A" attached to, and forming part of, this Order.

Kistruck chooses not to contest the proposed order and waives the procedural requirement under section 441(2) of the Act for a Notice of Intention to make an order and his right under section 441(3) to request a hearing.

TAKE NOTICE THAT pursuant to section 441(7) of the Act, AND WITH THE CONSENT OF KISTRUCK, the Superintendent hereby orders that Stuart Kistruck cease and desist from, directly or indirectly, engaging in the business of insurance or carrying on the business of insurance, or otherwise undertaking insurance on behalf of another person or as an insurer, an agent or an adjuster or an employee or representative of an insurer or an agent or an adjuster, for a period of two (2) years from the date of the Cease and Desist Order.

AND TAKE NOTICE THAT section 447(2)(b) of the Act provides that any person who fails to comply with any order made under the Act is guilty of an offence and liable on a first conviction to a fine of not more than $100,000 and on each subsequent conviction to a fine of not more than $200,000.

AND FURTHER TAKE NOTICE THAT section 447(4) of the Act provides

that every director, officer and chief agent of a corporation who caused, authorized, permitted or participated in a corporation committing an offence, or who fails to take reasonable care to prevent a corporation from committing an offence, is also guilty of an offence and is liable on a first conviction to a fine of not more than $100,000 and on each subsequent conviction to a fine of not more than $200,000.

ISSUED AT the City of Toronto this 31st day of January, 2007

Robert Christie
Chief Executive Officer and
Superintendent of Financial Services

SUPERINTENDENT OF FINANCIAL SERVICES

REGARDING the *Insurance Act*, R.S.O. 1990, c. I. 8, as amended, (the "Act") in particular section 441

AND REGARDING Stuart Kistruck ("Kistruck")

SCHEDULE "A" TO CEASE AND DESIST ORDER

1. For the purposes of these proceedings, Kistruck and the Superintendent of Financial Services agree to the following facts.
2. At the relevant time, Stuart Kistruck was President of Pilot Insurance, a position he had held since 1995, a period of eight years. Kistruck had been employed by Pilot since 1981.
3. Pilot had for some years had a reserving practice which Kistruck supported and in which he participated, which differed significantly from standard industry practice in that, among other things, it included a system of loss reserve banking. In late 2002 and early 2003, concerns about this practice, including a potential material shortfall in reserves for the year 2002 and prior, had been raised with Kistruck and within Pilot. Kistruck did not provide

Cease and Desist Order Against Stuart Kistruck ("Kistruck") - Financial Services Commis... Page 2 of 2

information about this practice and the concerns that had been raised, and did not personally ensure such information was provided, to the company's actuary or external auditors.

4. On February 28, 2003, Kistruck signed an affidavit verifying Pilot's Annual Return for the year ending December 31, 2002 (the "Original 2002 Return"), which was filed with the Superintendent on March 3, 2003. The affidavit certified that, in summary:

> the annual return was a full and correct report of all assets, liabilities, income expenditure and of the conditions and affairs of the insurer;

> the signatories were satisfied that the provision for unpaid claims and adjustment expenses was adequate to cover all costs of ultimate settlement of the claims.

5. The Original 2002 Return did not incorporate information concerning Pilot's reserving practices and/or reflect the concerns regarding unreserved losses that had been identified. Kistruck did not adequately investigate the concerns that had been raised prior to signing the Original 2002 Return, and did not ensure that the above information was incorporated in the Original 2002 Return. In signing and filing the Original 2002 Return, Kistruck furnished misleading or incomplete information to the Superintendent.

6. In early April 2003, Pilot informed the Superintendent that it had identified a material shortfall in claims reserving in respect of 2002 and prior year periods. Pilot subsequently filed a restated Annual Return for the year ending December 31, 2002, in which Pilot's reserves for the years 2002 and prior were materially increased.

7. Kistruck acknowledges that an insurance company's loss experience is a relevant factor in determining premiums charged to consumers and if losses are not fully recorded the company could be at financial risk.

Financial Services Commission of Ontario -
http://www.fsco.gov.on.ca/english/licensing/ceasedesistorders/cdo-kistruck.asp
© Queen's Printer for Ontario, 2006

CHAPTER SEVEN

Mystery and SCC Records

While my counsel was embroiled in discussions with the Supreme Court of Canada he hired a lawyer in Ottawa to visit the Supreme Court of Canada and review all of the evidence that was in the Court which included all the lower Court trial material as well as all of the material and file from the Court of Appeal for Ontario. His job was to find any reference to the name Chris Porter and report on his findings and provide copies of the pages in question. In a letter dated March 21, 2002 this Ottawa lawyer reported that the name Chris Porter appeared on the following pages however three crucial pages that would contradict the Supreme Court of Canada ruling were not identified, namely, pages 502, 548 and 596 of Volume 1 of the proceedings at trial in the Whiten v. Pilot Insurance Company record before the Court. They reported that on March 21, 2002, when we attended at the Supreme Court of Canada, we reviewed all records which were made available to us at that time. Ironically the one page that was made available was 104 of Volume 1 of the proceedings however the Supreme Court simply ignored this evidence about my role as described by Pilot Insurance Companies lower court lawyer.

On August 25, 2004 a discovery was found with astonishment at the Court of Appeal for Ontario, namely pages 502, 548 and 596 of Volume 1 of the proceedings at trial of Whiten v. Pilot Insurance Company. The material had been returned to the Court of Appeal of Ontario and pages were sent by me to the Ottawa lawyer in a letter dated September 5, 2004.

In response on October 27, 2004 my Ottawa lawyer advised that, "Unfortunately, the aforementioned pages which you have attached to your letters, were not available to us for inspection at the time we attended at the Supreme Court of Canada to inspect the records in the Whitens v. Pilot matter. Had those pages been provided to us by the Supreme Court of Canada we would have reported to your solicitor that your name appeared on those pages."

In a letter dated September 5, 2004, I wrote to my Ottawa lawyer and asked the following question. Further to your report of April 30, 2002, "My Toronto Lawyer had retained your services on my behalf to review the record documentation at the Supreme Court of Canada and look for any reference to my name in the above mentioned case. (Whiten v. Pilot SCC 27229)." At that time, the Supreme Court of Canada file and the Court of Appeal for Ontario and the Trial Proceedings records were together. You inspected the material at the Supreme Court of Canada on March 31, 2002. The material from both the Court of Appeal and the lower Court were not returned to the Court of Appeal for Ontario until April 22, 2002.

The Supreme Court of Canada was probably aware of the nature of my Ottawa lawyer's inspection and would have been aware that my name was mentioned several times in the material in question. I had called the Supreme Court of Canada on February 22, 2002 to complain about his name being used in the Supreme Court Judge's reasons for judgment. The Supreme Court of Canada informed me that at least three of their people reviewed all of the material before my Ottawa lawyer attended the Court. The Supreme Court of Canada needed to find out if the Supreme Court Judge was correct about calling me a senior claims manager. The Supreme Court of Canada was aware that my Ottawa lawyer was investigating for similar reasons.

I informed the Supreme Court of Canada that I had recently reviewed the record in Whiten v. Pilot Insurance Company at the

Court of Appeal for Ontario and discovered that my name was mentioned on three rather significant pages in Volume 1 of the Proceedings at Trial pages 502, 548, and 596. On page 596 the independent adjuster testifies in answer to a question posed on page 595. The Court of Appeal for Ontario has certified copies of these pages along with their record revealing that the material was at the Supreme Court of Canada. The question is whether the Ottawa lawyer missed these pages when he examined the record in the Supreme Court of Canada or was this material not made available by the Supreme Court of Canada for his inspection? It was unfortunate that it had taken me so many years to find and review that material. However when you are looking for what should have been obvious for the Supreme Court of Canada, one would not think that crucial evidence was being ignored and discarded.

On page 502 of the independent adjuster's discovery evidence, he testifies that when reporting to Pilot Insurance Company in Toronto, "it just goes to their head office, and then they designate the file. In this case, it turned out to be a fellow by the name of Chris Porter." However he is very specific about reporting to the Peterborough branch manager. This would have been significant for the Supreme Court Judge to help him understand how the rest of the reports after January 18, 1994 should have looked. On page 548 of the discovery evidence of the independent adjuster at the bottom paragraph he states that he discussed the February 3, 1994 report with the branch manager and not me. On this page you will see my name used twice and this is about the February 3, 1994 report." He does not know for sure if I received this report. The Supreme Court Judge does not understand from this testimony that the independent adjuster is discussing the February 3, 1994 report with the branch manager and not me.

The Supreme Court Judge had the Court of Appeal for Ontario and Trial Proceedings records and would have seen pages 595 and 596 of the independent adjuster's discovery evidence regarding the answer to the question the plaintiff's lawyer raised, regarding the 'train of thought'. The Supreme Court Judge told the world that it was the Senior Claims Manager, Chris Porter's 'train of thought' after learning about the Whitens financial problems. When the independent adjuster responds to the plaintiff's question about this issue when asked whether this was the Branch Manager's train of thought or Chris Porter's train of thought he answers that it was the Branch Manager's train of thought. The plaintiff's lawyer even asked the question of the independent adjuster, to rule out the possibility that I was in anyway in agreement with 'the branch manager's train of thought'. The plaintiff's lawyer wanted to know if it was only the branch manager's suspicion of the cause of the fire when he used the words 'as opposed' to Mr. Porter. The independent adjuster answers 'yes'. There was no evidence before the Court that I had a suspicion or a train of thought. I had never given evidence or even been questioned at examinations for discoveries or otherwise. In the plaintiff's lawyer's own words, I was not thought to be an issue as to what motivated Pilot Insurance Company to deny his client's claim.

This correspondence to the Ottawa lawyer was copied to the Registrar of the Supreme Court of Canada and the Canadian Judicial Council where I brought complaints regarding the Supreme Court of Canada and the Judge in question in the Whiten v. Pilot Insurance Judgment.

CHAPTER EIGHT

Critical Review of Evidence March 31, 2002

This was the first communication requested by the Registrar of the Supreme Court of Canada

The critical review of the evidence dated, March 31, 2002 is the analysis of the factums ordered from the Supreme Court of Canada in March 2002. My family and I met with the Registrar of the Supreme Court of Canada in August 2002 during which the Registrar requested a letter from me outlining all of the issues I had with the judgment in relation my concerns. After I received the factums from the Supreme Court of Canada in March 2002, I started to write a critical review of the factums.

APPELLANT'S FACTUM IN RESPONSE TO CROSS APPEAL

Para#9:

The May 11, 1995 letter from lower court lawyer for Pilot Insurance Company does not end as stated by Pilot in Paragraph 36 of its factum on the main appeal. It ends like this:

We need to get this resolved verbally and then in writing. I should note that Pilot has asked me to write this letter to get the concerns placed on the table in no uncertain terms to foster a good, strong approach to this matter.

Para#24:

The issue of subjective intent was never raised by Pilot at trial. Not only was it raised for the first time in the Court of Appeal, but also, as indicated earlier, Pilot refused to produce documents relevant thereto. Where a corporation puts it state of mind in issue, it is improper to shelter those documents, which disclose its true State of mind.

Para#25:

Before an appellate court will consider a new issue, it must be satisfied that it has before it a full evidentiary record. In this case, Pilot, by its refusal to produce relevant documents, has prevented a full record from being before this court.

APPELLANT'S FACTUM

Para#15:

Despite the unqualified conclusion that the fire was accidental, the manager of Pilot's Peterborough branch, instructed the independent adjuster to report the matter to the Insurance Crime Prevention Bureau ("ICPB"), whose response was included in a letter to Pilot dated February 25, 1994: "If we came into court with the engineering evidence and this probable cause, we wouldn't have a leg to stand on as far as declining the claim". At discovery, the branch manager's evidence was the ICPB's opinion didn't matter to Pilot and wasn't going to affect how it would handle this file."

Para#16:

On the same day that ICPB told Pilot it didn't have a leg to stand on, the independent adjuster wrote a further report: He had been conducting further investigation

Para#24:

The lower court lawyer wrote to Pilot's first engineer and cc: the branch manager and the claims manager for Pilot Insurance Company (who was not me)

"It tells him to ignore such facts as Mr. Whitens frostbite. The initial engineer had never received a letter like this in all his years of fire investigations. He was sufficiently concerned that Pilot's counsel was misunderstanding his analysis that he contacted Pilot's claims manager to suggest a meeting of everyone concerned where he could explain his opinion. Pilot never convened the meeting.

Para#26

"The June 9 letter is from counsel to the branch manager and Chris Porter, a senior claims examiner at Pilot's head office who was part of the committee decision to deny the claim".

There was not a committee to deny the fire claim. There was one meeting held by the executive claims staff to give direction to the new independent adjuster and the new engineer who were not hired by lower claims staff including the Senior Claims Examiner.

Para#29:

"The second engineer for Pilot Insurance conclusion was based on inaccurate information provided to him by Pilot's counsel in relation to the speed of the fire. The second engineer was never provided with the reports of the independent adjuster, who had actually interviewed the firefighters at the scene.

In fact none of the other experts hired by Pilot was provided with these reports. the first engineer, however, who later interviewed the firefighters, recognized that counsel's information was incorrect and corrected it on his copy of the letter"

"The above quote is from the Court of Appeal for Ontario and is a replica and not represented as an official version from Examinations for Discovery"

PILOT'S FACTUM

Para#36:

The lower court lawyer's May 11, 1995 letter did not instruct the second engineer for Pilot and the first engineer as to what their evidence ought to be, as the appellant's factum (30) suggests. Rather, the letter analyzed the differences between their respective theories as to how the fire progressed and exhorted them to resolve their differences. The letter did not ask the first engineer and the second engineer to ignore evidence, rather the lower court lawyer ended by stating:

> I am not sure we can maintain the credibility of either of you if we are left presenting a sort of mushy incoherent debate between the two of you with new scenarios coming to mind which are not supported by the evidence (emphasis added)

APPELLANT'S FACTUM

The following is how the appellant's factum records the May 11, 1995 letter mentioned above.

EXHIBIT 48

May 11, 1995 Letter from the lower court lawyer and the first engineer and the second engineer Para#30:

I am confident that each of you can destroy the credibility of the Whiten's engineer based on your discussions.

I am not sure we can maintain the credibility of either of you if we are left with presenting a sort of mushy, incoherent debate between the two of you with new scenarios coming to mind which are not supported by evidence. (Pilot's factum ends here). (The Appellants factum includes the following words at the end of the May 11, 1995 letter).

"We need to get this resolved verbally, and then in writing. I should note that Pilot have asked me to write this letter to get the concern placed on the table in no uncertain terms to foster a good strong approach to this matter"

It appears Pilot left this out when they presented their factum to the Court of Appeal, I wonder why?

ONTARIO COURT OF APPEAL FEBRUARY 5,1999

"Because of the Whitens' precarious financial situation and because he suspected arson, Pilot's claims manager asked the Insurance Crime Prevention Bureau, a body set up by The insurance industry, to investigate the fire. The Bureau reported on February 25, 1994 "we wouldn't have a leg to stand on as far as declining the claim"

Having asked for the Bureau's opinion, the claims manager then said he gave it no credence and refused to consider it in dealing with the Whitens' claim. No one from Pilot testified why the claims manager took this position.

> "the above quote from the Court of Appeal for Ontario
> and is a replica and not represented as an official
> version from the judgment"

Read in for discovery of the Peterborough branch manager November 28, 1995:

Page 125: Page 126/1 27 are handwritten numbers and the question is "All Right"? What kind of question is that?

Question:

Well, on February 25, 1994, the independent adjuster wrote a letter to Mr. Porter with a copy to you in which, in the second paragraph, the independent adjuster relates a conversation that he had with a representative of the Insurance Crime Prevention Bureau. In the second paragraph of that letter, he relates that the ICPB representative said that: "if you went into court, you being Pilot, went into court with the engineering evidence, you wouldn't have a leg to stand on" and I'm paraphrasing here, but I think that's the essence of what is said in that letter. Did you have that letter at the time you and Mr. Porter decided to consult counsel?

Answer:

I would assume so.

Question:

Okay. Did you disagree then with what was in that letter?

Answer:

I never put any credence to an opinion by the Insurance Crime Prevention Bureau on that matter.

Question:

You never put any credence to it?

Answer:

Well, you said a qualified professional. Etc . . . .

Page 127:

Question:

But my question is was it your view or Mr. Porter's view that what the IC what the representative of the ICPB said just didn't matter or it wasn't going to form part of the consideration of how the file should be handled?

Answer:

> That's correct

(This is not an answer to the question as to whether it was Mr. Porter's view. It would not have been Mr. Porter's answer. The branch manager never consulted with Mr. Porter about his view on this matter.)

Page 115 & 116:

Question:

> Who made the decision to retain the second adjuster?

Answer:

> I don't know

The lower court lawyer: the branch manager doesn't know. I can help. I suspect it was some—

> It was something was a committee decision with me involved in the committee. So in other words it wasn't any particular person. A discussion occurred as to who should be used including whether it should be the first independent adjuster.

> (after the first independent adjuster and the first engineer was hired all other services were hired by the AVP and VP of Claims)

Question:

> All right. When you say a committee decision, who were the members other then you on the committee?

The lower court lawyer:

> Well, let me use that term very loosely. It was not a committee but it was involved in it. It was Chris Porter, perhaps the AVP of claims had been consulted by

Mr. Porter, and I believe that is the case, and as well I think that the Vice President of Claims had also been consulted—consulted at that point as well about the appropriate approach to take in relation to further investigation, and eventually that decision was made to retain the services of the second independent adjuster.

(When I returned from his back operation it was the end of April 1994. I was not able to lift anything, still recovering from the effects of my operation, however on or about June 10, 1994 the A.V.P. of claims brought the Whiten claim to the examiner's desk along with the June 9, 1994 letter from the lower court lawyer. The AVP and the V.P. of Claims wanted a meeting arranged with the new independent adjuster, the lower court lawyer, internal investigator, and the new engineer. They discussed the case. This was the only time this group was assembled and it is therefore my contention that this was not a committee but rather a group discussion with the executive giving directions as to how the claim would be investigated.)

Page 147:

Question:
> Who made the decision to deny this claim?

The lower court lawyer:
> I would say it was the combination of Chris Porter, AVP and VP, in other words, the claimant's examiners and executives that you've heard about. I don't know how strongly the AVP of Claims was involved in it. You know, he might have been involved heavily: He might not have been other than on a consultative basis.

NOTE:
> (This makes it sound as though the Senior Management weren't involved. The only person who was identified in evidence to make the decision was the VP of Claims.)

67

Question:

> So you're suggesting that you have reason to believe his involvement was lesser then—well, not reason to believe but reason to suspect his involvement lesser then

The lower court lawyer:

> No his style is to be more in the background on files, and sometimes partway through you discovery that he's really got a hand in things that you didn't think of earlier—that you didn't think he had earlier.
>
> I know that he was aware of this matter. I know he was being consulted about it, and I'm presuming he was also a participant in the decision to deny the claim.

Question:

> Well, would you ask that question, please, who it was that made that decision to deny the claim?

The lower court lawyer:

> Yes

The lawyer for the plaintiff:

> and in answer to the question to the undertaking, the answer given was by letter dated October 4, 1995. The ultimate decision to deny the claim was the Vice President of Claims and Secretary for Pilot Insurance Company and possibly on the Board of Directors for General Accident (AVIVA).

(This is very important. An answer as to who denied the claim is given a year after being asked as to who denied the claim. The actual discovery was November 1994 of the Branch Manager of Peterborough. He and the lower court lawyer might have known who denied the claim. This decision was made by the V.P. of claims in June or July 1994 during a meeting at Pilot Insurance Company's Head Office. The lower court lawyer seems to be saying that he received this information by a letter dated October 4, 1995. Who was this letter from and why did it take a letter from the V.P. of Claims at Pilot Insurance Company to allow the lower Court lawyer to answer this question? Who at Pilot Insurance Company told the lower Court lawyer and Branch Manager not to answer this question at the Branch Manager's original Examination for Discovery? Could you imagine such a serious decision to be made with no paper trail to the person giving the order?)

"Was their a directing mind at Pilot Insurance Company or maybe even General Accident, AVIVA?"

Page 104:

> If Chris Porter was not a manager, not a decision maker, virtually no authority. Why would the lower Court lawyer put him on this committee as a decision maker? As an examiner Chris Porter position was as a coordinator, advisor, etc . . . Not part of the Directing minds of Pilot.

Answer:

> **Mr. Porter is an examiner. Virtually, he doesn't have the authority to settle, No signing authority.**

Question:

> All right. I don't want to guess here, but I'm presuming then that Mr. Porter's role is advisor. Would that be a fair description? In other words, he would receive reports from you and say to the AVP of Claims that in his view it's advisable to settle the matter for a certain figure and then the AVP of Claims would authorize that. Is that the way it works?

Answer:

> Yes

Question:

> Or the AVP of Claims may not authorize it for whatever his reasons are?

Answer:
>Correct.

Question:
>To whom does the AVP of Claims report or seek authority?

Answer:

>The Vice President of Claims and Secretary of Pilot Insurance Company

>"the above quote from the Court of Appeal for Ontario and is a replica and not represented as an official version from examinations for discoveries"

Supreme Court Judgment: February 22, 2002

Para#7:
>The independent adjuster made further investigations during which he determined that although The Whitens' mortgage payments were in arrears, refinancing was being arranged. It appears that Pilot's senior claims manager, Mr. Chris Porter, Was already moving towards the conclusion that the claim should be disputed based on his suspicions of the families financial problems. In a letter dated February 25, 1994, the independent adjuster wrote to Pilot . . . .

Para#9:
>Pilot requested that the Insurance Crime Prevention Bureau, a body set Up by the insurance industry to review the analysis of Pilot's investigator by letter dated February 25, 1994, the Bureau reported that "we wouldn't Have a leg to stand on as far as declining the claim. Pilot having asked for the opinion, then apparently decided that the Bureau's investigator was not in fact qualified to render an opinion. No one from Pilot testified as to why the claims

examiner and subsequently Pilot's Branch Manager, (BLANK), rejected this advice as well.

"the above quote from the Supreme Court judgment is a replica and not represented as an official version from the judgment"

RESPONDENT'S RECORD—FACTUM ON APPEAL

"The independent adjuster's report of February 3, 1994 indicates that he had already asked the ICPB to investigate, as he was instructed to do by the manager of Pilot's Peterborough branch office manager, (BLANK)."

(We do not know what was contained in the February 17, 1994 report from the independent adjuster, we only know that it was about 17 pages in length and was about the Whitens contents claim. It also had a covering letter).

It should be noted, that there was no evidence of my complicity or that I would have gone along with any alleged improprieties on the part of the lower Court lawyer for Pilot Insurance Company or the engineers and adjusters. There was no evidence that I was involved in the decision for the lower Court lawyer acting for Pilot Insurance Company, to take the independent adjuster's file prior to the trial. I always believed that the engineer Pilot Insurance Company engaged was telling the truth and that his evidence was unblemished.

At the time of this claim I was an examiner for Pilot Insurance Company and involved with about 300 to 400 hundred claims. This claim did not have significance to cause the type of reaction it received my senior management. The AVP and the V.P. of Claims were my superiors and at that time had a great many years more experience. Until this claim became an issue I had no reason to doubt the credibility and judgment of my superiors.

There was an expression of concern from the claims manager that was raised when the possibility of his name might be associated with the Whiten fire claim. The claims manager assured me that this was a senior management file and it would be the responsibility of senior management to deal with any problems that could result from their decisions. My role was limited to being the examiner on the claim not the decision maker.

On March 1, 2002 I sent a letter to the Registrar of the Supreme Court of Canada stating that, "I am protesting the facts of the case as proposed by a justice of the Supreme Court. It would seem his desire to mention me directly as the catalyst of the denial of this claim has caused serious harm to me and is a wrong assumption. I pleaded with my manager and Assistant Vice President to allow me to attend the original trial however my request was turned down. Every person associated with this claim knows I did not propose that the claim be denied. Even the independent adjuster was aware of my involvement. I was an examiner taking directions from my superiors not initiating any information that would draw the conclusion the Supreme Court Judge has proposed. I can only imagine someone is attempting to either avoid taking the responsibility for themselves or for some other sinister reason. My lawyer has suggested I request the factums submitted from all applicants mentioned on the list attached. Once I have this information, I can then have my lawyer investigate who mislead the Supreme Court of Canada and the justice of the Supreme Court who wrote the decision. I can tell you that the decision to include my name in the judgment has already cost me a promotion in my company and I may be fired. This is very serious to me as I am the only bread winner in my family".

Finally, we go back to our original concern about the absent page from the discovery transcript of the branch manager for Pilot Insurance Company, namely page 101. This along with the following should be brought to the attention of the Supreme Count of Canada should you think it advisable. We have raised a concern about pages 1264, 1265 and 1266 that they do not match. If you notice on the documents received from the Supreme Court of Canada, pages 126 & 127 are hand written and when page 128 begins the answer does not follow 127. The Peterborough branch manager never answers an important question from the insured's lawyer, namely whether I agree with his opinion on the ICPB report. Secondly, page 1239 goes into details about the A.V.P. of Claims for Pilot Insurance Company and his role at Pilot Insurance Company. The court of appeal lawyer for Pilot Insurance never submits this page; unless the Supreme Court of Canada neglected to send me a copy.

This page is identified in the fax material I sent to you as page 1239 read-in of the Tuesday, November 28, 1995 evidence of the branch manager of the AVP of Claims for Pilot Insurance Company. The Supreme Court of Canada would have numbered this page as page **101.**

In the end and as an undesirable last resort, I made an application with the Canadian Judicial Council asking for a review of the Supreme Court Judge's reasons with respect to my name being used in this judgment. The Chief Justice of The Supreme Court is also the head of the Canadian Judicial Council which is the only avenue open for a complaint involving a Supreme Court Judge.

As previously stated I previously contacted the Prime Minister, the Justice Department, Human Rights Commission, the Premier of Ontario, Attorney General and other officials in both the Government of Canada and the Government of Ontario trying to find direction and an answer as to why the law and the Charter of Freedoms did not protect an innocent person who had never been able to face his accuser, the Supreme Court of Canada and the Judge who wrote the decision.

CHAPTER NINE

Canadian Judicial Council

The Chief Justice of Manitoba and Chairperson of the Judicial Conduct Committee of the Council reviewed my complaints twice, once before he was aware of the evidence found in the Ontario Court of Appeal and once after. In both instances the Chief Justice of Manitoba and Chairperson of the Judicial Conduct Committee of the Council, responded to my complaints as follows;

"In your correspondence you again express your concerns about the Judge's description of your role in his reasons for decision in Whiten v. Pilot Insurance Company. You allege that in his decision, the Judge erroneously described you as a decision-maker in the handling of the insured's claim. Moreover, you allege he did this on purpose to avoid blaming those who were actually responsible.

As was stated in the Council's earlier correspondence to you dated January 19, 2004, Chief Justice of Manitoba recognizes and understands your concerns about what you take to be a serious error in the Supreme Court Judge's reasons. However, as stated previously an error in a judge's decision—and again Chief Justice of Manitoba makes no comment on this with regard to the Supreme Court Judge's decision—is not a judicial conduct matter. As the material you provided establishes no basis for a finding of misconduct, Chief Justice of Manitoba advises that this file will remain closed."

Of course the one defence the Supreme Court Judge has in his reasons is that he never completes the sentence, namely, that Chris Porter denied the Whitens claim.

Soon after the Supreme Court of Canada released its reason for Judgment a Quebec law firm posted a communiqué on their website and sent hard copies to the insurance industry announcing that I was the Senior Claims Manager who denied the Whitens fire claim. The question is, why was the inaccurate account of my title and role described by this law firm especially if it was posted after the Supreme Court of Canada announced changes to my title?

It turned out that the insurance company that insured this law firm from Quebec was AVIVA. Therefore while providing coverage for the law firm, were they not in a position to know the truth about my role and title. The questions is, why did AVIVA fight me all the way to trial before their insured conceded that they were wrong and apologize and why did AVIVA avoid this same gesture?

The only other organization that became relevant in this matter was an organization called AIDWYC, Association in Defence of the Wrongly Convicted. However it should be understood that this volunteer organization's only mandate is with those wrongly convicted of murder and they do not have the mandate, funding or otherwise to take on issues which pertain to matters outside this enormously important human injustice in Canada. However its director has become a respected friend for understanding and support for me over this dilemma. Although it is not the same as being imprisoned inside the confines of a building the confinement to one's life when wrongly libeled by the highest Court in the land can be just as damaging. It is my hope that the clarification of this case has been accurately and honestly described and it is not written to wrongly accuse anyone other than to point out a serious flaw in our justice system that is systemic. I have gone to great lengths to protect the names of those involved however I cannot control how this case is promoted by others including the Supreme Court of Canada.

In this analysis of this Supreme Court of Canada ruling, I have tried to understand and convey to the reader an understanding of what transpired in what the Supreme Court of Canada findings describe about me and the use of my name, role and title. I have also attempted to convey an analysis of the actions of the lawyers and insurance companies that I believe assisted the Supreme Court of Canada with those findings. How do you challenge a Supreme Court of Canada ruling after the decisions are made?

CHAPTER TEN

Supreme Court of Canada Right to Use My Name?

The Supreme Court of Canada, as revealed in paragraph 7 of their ruling, decided to focus the attention of the judgment on me and associating undesirable labels such as 'Rogue', 'Delinquent' which were published in hard copy and on the Internet by at least three leading Internet publishers who track all Supreme Court of Canada decisions. The decision was also published in print and is one of the most referenced cases in Canadian history. Clearly the Supreme Court of Canada should have realized that the publication would damage me to the point where I would suffer for the rest of my life. The Supreme Court of Canada, Registrar's office, Chief Justice etc. have been asked for years to explain why my name was used and to be allowed to defend myself even unrepresented by a lawyer.

The Chief Justice and the Supreme Court of Canada will only advise that the case is closed and no explanation will be given and I do not have a right to be heard. This is by far the harshest punishment ever inflicted upon a person who has never been tried. This is unprecedented and the Supreme Court of Canada know that if they open the door even a inch to have the ruling assessed by an independent Judge on the merits of their findings regarding my role they would lose.

What would have happened if the Supreme Court of Canada Condemned an Executive at Pilot Insurance Company rather than a lowly employee?

The unthinkable might have happened. That person would have actually been a corporate entity an officer and director of the corporation Pilot Insurance Company and its parent company AVIVA. Do the words "Rainmaker" bring back thoughts of a landmark decision in the United States that brought down an entire company? Therefore did the Supreme Court of Canada make a mistake and was it potentially negligent and therefore did the damages fit the crime? In the Supreme Court Judge's ruling he suggests that it was not a problem for me to have a train of thought but that it was wrong to have that train of thought with no evidence to support that train of thought and that I prolonged the decision not to change that train of thought long after the claim should have been paid. In other words I maintained a train of thought and was in a position to change that train of thought and convince my executives to pay the claim.

I do not understand how the Supreme Court of Canada arrived at their conclusions about me in their ruling. Were the mistakes made because of the inferences made by the Supreme Court of Canada or were those inferences fostered in Pilot's factum to the Supreme Court of Canada? Surely the inferences were not made simply for the purposes of defending the decision to convince the reader?

Perhaps I actually recommended that the claim be paid from the beginning and at various times including before the trial began, however since the Supreme Court Judge and the other Justices of Supreme Court of Canada did not want to hear from the person they were condemning before or after the ruling was pronounced, the idea of another side to the proposition was never considered. This is considered in philosophical terms irrational. A reasonable person will always want to understand as many sides to a proposition as possible to assure its accuracy. In philosophical terms when ever you affirm a proposition you negate the opposite position to the proposition.

In the end had the Justices of the Supreme Court of Canada considered the evidence I might have presented, they might have been exposed to another side to the propositions pronounced by the author of the Supreme Court ruling. Why were they so content to avoid this normally important step in achieving a rational decision that would support the concept of justice fairness etc.?

It would have been obvious to the Supreme Court of Canada that the evidence before them lacked, what would have been key testimonial evidence from me. So making an inference about me would have been the next best answer to avoid any possible conflict in their ruling.

Who would care whether I was afforded any rights when the Supreme Court of Canada did not care. No other Government entity in the Canadian Government or Ontario Government cared about how an innocent citizen of Canada with an unblemished 23 year career in insurance claims having worked for no less than 5 major insurance companies involved with thousands of claims in that period of time, was laid out and condemned by the Supreme Court of Canada. In all that time my name had never been mentioned in any court proceeding in this or any other country in the world. However they certainly all know my name now.

CHAPTER ELEVEN

Supreme Court of Canada's Punishment of Pilot Insurance Company

In it's factum to the Court of Appeal for Ontario, Pilot does not mention my name however my name is mentioned three times in it's factum to the Supreme Court of Canada. At the same time Pilot's factum avoids focusing attention on the lower Court lawyer. Was this deliberate because it might look as though Pilot was attempting to avoid taking responsibility for his conduct to deflect criticism might backfire? This might have compelled the Court of Appeal for Ontario and the Supreme Court of Canada to conclude Pilot's conduct was deliberate and therefore the idea of using the lower Court lawyer as a scapegoat might undermine the argument that the award was excessive. Would this focus to deflect attention to a former employee, to be used as a **Scapegoat**, entail the same concern?

Clearly this was being discussed with the V.P. of Claims for Pilot Insurance Company and the executives at Pilot Insurance Company and General Accident. The idea of deflecting attention was already being prepared and was evident in the changes in the Court of Appeal for Ontario factum. Was the change in the factum designed to deflect attention to a lowly employee whose identity was being saved until a possible appeal to the Supreme Court of Canada, where the stakes increased dramatically?

Therefore when it came time for Pilot Insurance Company to prepare it's factum and mention my name three times to the

Supreme Court of Canada, they realized that the same concern for deflecting attention to the lower Court lawyer was not as serious as a lowly employee who no longer worked for Pilot Insurance Company.

It was evident by the use of my name in it's factum that Pilot Insurance Company did not have a moral sense of duty when they exposed my name in a manner that could deflect attention away from the corporation and those who were in positions of authority and who were responsible for the corporation.

Therefore it is difficult to know whether Pilot Insurance Company received a punishment that fit the accusations alleged by the Supreme Court of Canada although the Supreme Court of Canada had a right to punish Pilot Insurance Company. However with the mistake made by the Supreme Court of Canada did this allow Pilot Insurance Company to deflect attention to a lowly employee and create a more senior position to complete the ensemble, it is hard to understand how any sanction would fit the punishment. Was Pilot out to avoid a possible rainmaker ruling or to avoid embarrassment? (The Rainmaker is a 1995 fictional novel by John Grisham depicting a landmark insurance claim where the jury awarded a multi-million dollar settlement for punitive damages). Perhaps Pilot was aware of this fictional novel and concerned about fiction becoming reality.

When I informed the Supreme Court of Canada that the ruling with my name still on the Internet referenced by so many cases and lawyers in the legal community, that this was causing severe harm to my life and that of my family, I was told by representatives of the Supreme Court of Canada they were not interested. The matter is closed. We will not allow you to speak with any of us and we will not ever hear your arguments.

The Supreme Court of Canada would not respond to receiving the manuscript for this book which was sent to them several times. That is the height of justice in Canada the worst demonstration of injustice in any free and democratic country. This is clearly a systemic problem and it is ignored by all levels of Government in Canada.

The final question for this book has to do with what we learned from the Al Capone methodology and whether those lessons continue to haunt the fabric of our society. I was simply an employee minding my own business raising a family and for 23 years had a perfect working record in the insurance industry where I am now blackballed and banned by the very industry I once supported.

The Supreme Court of Canada want me to desist and to stop annoying them with complaints about my life being ruined by their mishandling of my identity. Perhaps this is just an isolated incident in the reasons for judgment in Whiten v. Pilot Insurance Company SCC 27229 or is it a systemic problem that supported an aberration from the lower Court in the Punitive Damage award of the Superior Court of Ontario?

The Supreme Court of Canada wants to protect the integrity of the Court and their decision. Therefore admitting an error in judgment in one aspect of the judgment might affect other conclusions. Admitting to an error regarding the misuse of my name and my identity might point to an arrogant attitude of the Court.

The following exemplifies just how specific the Supreme Court of Canada was in their wording in the ruling, when dealing with the identity of the actual Claims Manager for Pilot Insurance Company, where he could have been identified in the ruling. As a courtesy and to be consistent with protecting the identity of others in this book, in this case I have used the word 'Blank' in place of the Claims Manager's actual name.

The following is from the appellant's factum to the Supreme Court of Canada, page 8; "On May 4, 1994 Pilot's legal counsel wrote to the branch manager with copies to the branch manager, (BLANK) and the Claims Manager, (BLANK) at Pilot's Head Office." (Blank was the Claims Manager of Pilot Insurance Company), "The letter consists of five pages setting out in detail factors to be considered by the expert. This was the first of sixteen letters written or copied to the first engineer by Pilot's counsel. It also tells him to ignore such facts as Mr. Whitens' frostbite. The first engineer had never received a letter like this in all his years of fire investigations. He was sufficiently concerned that Pilot's counsel was misunderstanding his analysis that he contacted Pilot's Claims Manager to suggest a meeting of everyone concerned where he could explain his opinion. Pilot never convened the meeting." How does the Supreme Court Judge not recognize who the Claims Manager is when his name is being used in that correspondence and how did this submission by the lawyer acting for Mr. & Mrs. Whiten become a communication with me?

On page 9 paragraph 22 of the Respondent's factum to the Supreme Court of Canada, Pilot Insurance Company describes these letters in a different way leaving out the name of the Claims Manager, a person still employed with Pilot Insurance Company at the time, as follows:

"During the cross-examination of Pilot's first engineer, the trial judge ordered the production of a series of letters written by Pilot's lower court lawyer beginning May 4, 1994. Some of these letters were written to Pilot and copied to the first engineer (and, after they were retained, to the other two defence expert witnesses, engineers (BLANK) and the fire inspector (BLANK). Others were written to the expert witnesses and copied to Pilot. The May 4, 1994 letter began by stating that the author had spoken to a "quite seasoned and well-qualified firefighter."

What Pilot's factum clearly leaves out is any reference to the Claims Manager and the name (BLANK of that Manager), who happened to be the Claims Manager. Perhaps the Supreme Court of Canada, thought Chris Porter was the Senior Claims Manager over the Claims Manager and that he played an insignificant role such that he would never be called to testify or give evidence at Examinations for Discovery? However it was quite clear that I was not the claims manager or senior claims manager.

This is how the Supreme Court of Canada deal with the fact that the Claims Manager is identified by the Whitens' lawyer in the same paragraph in his factum to the Supreme Court of Canada regarding the letters to the first Pilot engineer from Pilot's lower court lawyer including the May 4, 1994 letter in paragraphs 13 and 14 of the reasons for judgment:

"13 Pilot also retained an engineering expert, (BLANK). His initial report was made on January 28, 1994. In that report, he concluded that the fire was accidental. He gave two further reports in which he stated the same opinion. This engineer then received a letter dated May 4, 1994 from the respondent's trial counsel, Pilot's lower court lawyer, which adverted the arson theory:

One wonders whether the Whitens', even if they did not set the fire, sat back and allowed it to achieve a level that was convenient to them.

We need to be on top of this matter and to do it quickly. The other side has retained a lawyer and they are making noises of bad faith. The matter has to be revisited in its entirety, stripped down to the bare facts and rebuilt.

14 Pilot's first engineer (BLANK) concluded that he may have been misunderstood. He requested meeting but did not get one at the time. The jury must have concluded that he had not provided the opinion his client wanted to hear."

Why does the Supreme Court of Canada avoid identifying the Claims Manager as identified in the appellant's factum and instead quote Pilot's factum that does not identify the name of the Claims Manager? Throughout the reasons for judgment it is rarely seen where the Justices of the Supreme Court of Canada do not use some reference to my name in their condemnation of Pilot Insurance Company. Here they have the Claims Manager mentioned and yet my name is not used in reference. Perhaps it is because they know that (BLANK) is the Claims Manager and any reference to him would not be acceptable to the Executives of Pilot Insurance Company or General Accident?

The "Al Capone method is alive and well with the executives at Pilot Insurance Company and AVIVA, in fact the Executive Vice President in charge of claims and secretary and possibly on the Board of Directors for General Accident wrote an article misquoting a Court of Appeal Justice who ruled in the Court of Appeal trial when he reveals his desire to focus attention on me, the Supreme Court of Canada responded in accordance with his proclamation.

The Vice President of Claims for Pilot is quoted as stating the following;

> "A quote from the Justice of the Court of Appeal in his findings at the Court of Appeal" . . . there is nothing in the evidence to suggest that the conduct so rightly condemned was the product of a corporate strategy by the appellant insurer to avoid payment of all policy claims or to discourage it's insured's from making claims. Nor, is there any suggestion that the defendant had profited by its actions. Rather, it appears to be an isolated instance . . .".

I am offended and angered by the "license" exercised by the press, but I guess that's what sells newspapers.

I look forward to your continued support in this matter.

Yours very truly,
Executive Vice President"

What that Court of Appeal Justice actually said in his reasons in paragraph 62 ends as follows; "Rather, it appears to have been an isolated instance for which the appellant's trial counsel should take full responsibility,"

> the above quote from the Court of Appeal for Ontario
> is a replica and not represented as an official version of
> the judgment

The Executive Vice President of Claims has misquoted the Justice of the Ontario Court of Appeal and was this a deliberate demonstration of a mastermind who may have influenced the outcome of a Supreme Court of Canada Judgment from the sidelines?

There remain many websites where both versions of the Supreme Court of Canada ruling can be found such as http://scc-csc.lexum.com/scc-csc/scc-csc/en/item/1956/index.do, http://www.peelinstitute.com/Links/links laws.html who have never asked for my permission to disclose my name who are protected by the Supreme Court of Canada. However early on a law firm in New Brunswick, were discovered posting an article entitled "Landmark decision serves as a wakeup call to insurance industry February 28, 2002. My lawyer identified certain allegations that might have been correlated to me and therefore requested that the article be reposted with a clarification and apology with respect to this error. It was obvious that the error was directly related to how the judgment was written by the Supreme Court Judge and exemplifies how the Supreme Court of Canada can be responsible for errors in judgment. The law firm in question responded quickly to correct their website and was big enough to apologize as follows:

"The original version of this commentary that appeared on this website contained words to the effect that Mr. Chris Porter, in the course of his employment as a claims examiner at Pilot Insurance Company, acted in an inappropriate and unprofessional manner in that he took a position that was not justified by the facts, and stated that the claimants, (Mr. & Mrs. Whiten), had been involved in two previous fires. Subsequent to the original publication of the case comment, we have ascertained and now recognize that there was no foundation to these allegations, and we regret that they were ever made. Our review of the reported decisions of the Trial Court, the Ontario Court of Appeal and the Supreme Court of Canada, revealed that the above noted conduct and comment referring to the 'two previous" fires was improperly attributed to Mr. Chris Porter. In fact, the Court specifically attributed this comment to an individual other than Mr. Porter. We are happy to take the earliest opportunity of correcting our error and of expressing to Mr. Chris Porter our sincere regret for any distress or embarrassment caused to him by the publication of the original case comment."

This apology came as a result of comments of an analysis made by this law firm regarding of the Supreme Court of Canada ruling in Whiten v. Pilot Insurance Company. The analysis of the senior New Brunswick law firm commented in the following paragraphs had included a connection to the allegation to the Claims Manager that was wrongly determined to be Chris Porter in the original Supreme Court of Canada ruling.

"The Whitens home burnt on January 18, 1994 and Mrs. Whiten, her husband and daughter barely escaped in their nightclothes. The temperature was—18 Celsius. They lost everything including their three cats. The firefighters at the scene and the fire chief later investigating the blaze found no evidence of arson. Both Mr. and Mrs. Whiten were unemployed and, of course, had financial problems. Mortgage payments were in arrears but their lawyer informed the insurance company that refinancing was in place. Pilot Insurance hired its own investigator, who concluded the fire was accidental and recommended payment of the claim.

Pilot fired him and replaced him with another adjuster. Pilot also hired an engineer whose first report concluded: accidental fire. The company went to the Insurance Crime Prevention Bureau to have them review the findings to date and the Bureau reported: ". . . we wouldn't have a leg to stand on as far as declining the claim."

Pilot decided the bureau's expert wasn't qualified to make the recommendation and for at least the fourth known time, the company refused to pay. For the next two years, Pilot continued to refuse to pay the claim on the hope the Whitens would settle for a much reduced amount. Mr. and Mrs. Whiten even offered to take a lie detector test as to their lack of involvement in arson but the company refused the offer. Pilot believed they had evidence to establish the Whitens involvement in two previous fires. At trial, it was determined this information was incorrect and could have been confirmed with minimal effort."

The above quote is still on the website of the law firm of the Province of New Brunswick along with the apology and clarification of Chris Porter's involvement. No lawsuit was ever initiated to resolve this issue however it was clear that the firm did not want to associate their article with Chris Porter. The question remains why the Supreme Court of Canada cannot be as gracious and just.

Roger McConchie a lawyer with the firm McConchie Law in Vancouver has been following the lawsuit with Robinson Sheppard Shapiro and provides the following analysis of the outcome of that matter and the matter of Chris Porter and the Supreme Court of Canada:

"2005 January11
Porter v Robinson Sheppard Shapiro, Court of Appeal for Ontario, Docket: C421 57, reversing 2004 June 29, Ontario Superior Court of Justice File No. 03-CV-243741 CM2

The Ontario Court of Appeal held that the evidentiary basis before the lower court judge was not sufficient to resolve the issue whether posting on the defendant law firm's website of a communiqué summarizing a judgment of the Supreme Court of

Canada in *Whiten v Pilot Insurance Co.* (2002), 209 DLR (4th) 257 was a publication on an occasion of qualified privilege.

In *Whiten,* the Supreme Court of Canada reversed a decision of the Ontario Court of Appeal and reinstated a $1 million jury award of punitive damages against an insurance company for bad faith denial of an insurance claim, in the process defining the basis on which punitive damages may be awarded by Canadian courts.

The lower court judge, whose summary judgment decision was reversed, had concluded that that defendant law firm had a duty, at least to their clients, to communicate the information, stating: *"The Internet is probably the least expensive and most efficient means of conveying this information, not only to existing clients, but to potential clients, and to the insurance community, all of which have a reciprocal interest with the defendant in receiving the information."*

A settlement of this libel action during the third day of trial means that the issue of qualified privilege for website postings will not reach the Court of Appeal for determination in this case.

[NOTE: Although Chris Porter was mentioned in the Supreme Court of Canada's judgment in *Whiten v Pilot Insurance,* Chris Porter was not the Pilot Insurance employee who denied Daphne Whitens insurance claim against Pilot nor was he in fact personally guilty of any bad faith towards Whiten. Chris Porter was not even called to testify at the trial in *Whiten v Pilot Insurance.* Chris Porter settled his libel action against the law firm on the third day of the trial. The settlement agreement contains certain terms which cannot be publicized on the Internet. Chris Porter has been unsuccessful so far in attempts to have the Supreme Court of Canada clarify certain passages in its judgment to make Chris Porter's non-involvement clear to readers unfamiliar with the detailed evidence placed before the trial court.]"

"Injustice anywhere is a threat to justice everywhere."

Martin Luther King Jr., *Letter from Birmingham Jail,*
April 16, 1963 US black civil rights leader & clergyman
(1929-1968)

Does this sermon have any relevance to the case of Chris Porter v. the Supreme Court of Canada? Should I not have a legal right to pursue the Supreme Court and perhaps the justice who wrote the decision?

The following document below is the April 11, 2002 letter from Anne Roland, Registrar of the Supreme Court of Canada to my lawyer, announcing that the Court issued revised reasons for judgment on April 10, 2002 indicating that paragraph 7 of the English version of the reasons, the title of Chris Porter had been changed to "Senior Claims Examiner" and that the change was made also in the French version.

Following that letter are 14 pages of evidence we found at the Court of Appeal for Ontario while my wife and I were examining the boxes returned to the Court of Appeal for Ontario from the Supreme Court of Canada after they waited a period of time after the April 11, 2002 letter. We examined the material for about two weeks at which point the Court of Appeal for Ontario certified and date stamped the copies we had made, August 24-25, 2004 and September 1, 2004.

Supreme Court of Canada
Registrar

Cour suprême du Canada
Registraire

April 11, 2002

Mr. Gordon A. Meiklejohn
Brannan Meiklejohn Butts LLP
262 Avenue Road
Toronto, Ontario
M4V 2G7

APR 17 2002

Dear Mr. Meiklejohn,

      RE: *Whiten v. Pilot Insurance Company*
              File 27229

This will confirm that I have received your letter of March 22, 2002, concerning the reasons for judgment in the above noted file.

The Court issued revised reasons for judgment on April 10, 2002, a copy of which is enclosed for your records. You will note that, at paragraph 7 of the English version of the reasons the title of Chris Porter has been changed to "Senior Claims Examiner." A corresponding change was made in the French version.

All legal publishers have been informed that the reasons are revised. The electronic version accessible through links at the Supreme Court of Canada web site has been updated.

Please do not hesitate to contact me if you have any questions about this.

Yours truly,

Anne Roland,
Registrar

cc. Gary R. Will
    Earl A. Cherniak, Q.C.
    Neil Finkelstein
    Robert B. Munroe

301 rue Wellington Street Ottawa (Ontario) K1A 0J1
Tel / Tél (613) 996-9277 · Fax / Télec : (613) 996-9138

Materials Sent to Supreme Court of Canada

C 23973   SCC 27229

Title of Proceedings: _WHITEN, DAPHNE V PILOT INSURANCE CO AND_
                                                              DEREK FRANCIS

Date: _DEC. 18-1998_

Book Materials	Judge's Names
	FINLAYSON, JA
APPEAL BOOK:	TWO - VOL I & II
SUPP APP BOOK:	
APPELLANT FACT:	ONE
RESPONDENT FACT:	ONE
OTHER MATERIALS :	FACTUM OF APPELLANT BY CROSS-APPEAL — ONE

TRANSCRIPTS:
date:

NOV 7 -98	TRIAL PROCEEDINGS
JAN 13 -98	TRIAL PROCEEDINGS
JAN 8- 98	VOL 1 -2 -3 -4 -5

CERTIFIED TO BE A TRUE AND CORRECT COPY OF THE ORIGINAL GIVEN UNDER MY HAND AND THE SEAL OF THIS COURT
COPIE AUTHENTIQUE CERTIFIÉE ET CONFORME À L'ORIGINAL
EN FOI DE QUOI, J'AI SIGNÉ ET APPOSÉ LE SCEAU DE CETTE COUR

THIS _1ST_ DAY OF _Sept_ 20 _04_

FAITLE _____ 20 ___

REGISTRAR / GREFFIER
COURT OF APPEAL FOR ONTARIO
COUR D'APPEL DE L'ONTARIO

104

1242
Tuesday, November 28, 1995

	resolve the claim?
ANSWER:	Mr. Porter is an examiner. Virtually, he doesn't have the authority to settle, no signing authority.
QUESTION:	All right. I don't want to guess here, but I'm presuming then that Mr. Porter's role is advisor. Would that be a fair description? In other words, he would receive reports from you and say to Mr. Hamilton that in his view it's advisable to settle the matter for a certain figure and then Mr. Hamilton would authorize that. Is that the way it works?
ANSWER:	Yes.
QUESTION:	Or Mr. Hamilton may not authorize it for whatever his reasons are?
ANSWER:	Correct."

Page 19:
"QUESTION 120: To whom does Mr. Hamilton report or seek authority?

ANSWER:	Mr. Cliff Jones.
QUESTION:	And who is he?
ANSWER:	He's the executive vice president and secretary.

Jan 18/94
10.31 a

Phoned insured
house is gutted.
He is staying at friends.
He had his pet cat in
D/S allowed outside.
Fire started in the back half
of the house. Origin of fire
not known. No nearby water save
firemen etc.

DATE: Jan 18/94

TO: Peterborough _____ 738.5141

FROM: Oshawa

RE: _____ Jay.

COMMENTS: New claim

Rob Francis
appointed Jan 18/94
11.40 pm

133

EX. 10 12

Inter**Spect**
National Claim Service

**FRANCIS, LABRASH, QUIBELL & ASSOCIATES
INSURANCE ADJUSTERS INC.**
Bobcaygeon   P.O. Box 972
Bobcaygeon, Ont. K0M 1A0
Tel: (705) 738-5141   Fax: (705) 738-5142

PRELIMINARY CLAIM NOTICE

PILOT INSURANCE COMPANY
2-223 Aylmer St. N.,
Peterborough, Ontario
K9J 3K4

DATE January 19, 1994

YOUR POLICY P00911982

YOUR FILE ~~Above~~ 94 L04/...

OUR FILE 1505-B

ATTN: Steve Carter

CC: Pilot Insurance Co. - Toronto

AGENCY James Insurance
              Brokers

We have received instructions   January 18, 1994   to
investigate a claim as follows.

TYPE OF CLAIM Fire - Building - Contents - ALE

INSURED Keith Whiten &
         Daphne Whiten

ADDRESS R.R.#2
           Haliburton, Ont.

ITEM INSURED Dwelling

COVERAGE Building $ 157,000
          Contents $ 117,750
          Deductible $ 200

EXPIRY DATE January 22 /94

THIRD PARTY   ADDRESS

DATE OF LOSS January 18/94
              1:15 a.m.

LOCATION Lots 5 & 6,
          Concession 2
          Dysart Township

TENTATIVE RESERVE Building $ 157,000
                   Contents $ 117,750
                   A.L.E. $ 20,000

REMARKS Fire destroyed insured's home and all the contents
         contained therein.

         Investigation Underway.

CERTIFIED TO BE A TRUE AND CORRECT
COPY OF THE ORIGINAL GIVEN UNDER
MY HAND AND THE SEAL OF THIS COURT
COPIE AUTHENTIQUE CERTIFIÉE ET
CONFORME À L'ORIGINAL.
EN FOI DE QUOI, J'AI SIGNÉ ET APPOSÉ
LE SCEAU DE CETTE COUR

ADJUSTER .... THIS 1ST DAY OF Sept. 2004

FAIT LE   20

REGISTRAR / GREFFIER

Inter**Spect**

95

EX. 12   122

YOUR FILE   94L0410
OUR FILE   1505-B

February 3, 1994

PILOT INSURANCE COMPANY
90 Eglington Ave.,
Toronto, Ontario
M4P 1E9

ATTN: Chris Porter

CC: Steve Carter

Dear Sir,

THIS WILL ACKNOWLEDGE DIRECT ASSIGNMENT RECEIVED AND THE FOLLOWING
ARE DETAILS OF OUR INVESTIGATION TO DATE.

INSURED: Keith Whiten & Daphne Whiten
          R.R.#2
          Haliburton, Ontario

COVERAGE: Building $ 157,000
           Contents $ 117,750
           Deductible $ 200

EXPIRY DATE: January 22, 1994

DATE OF LOSS: January 18, 1994

TYPE OF CLAIM: Fire - Building - Contents - A.L.E.

LOSS

     Further to my preliminary claim notice of January 19, 1994,
please be advised that upon receipt of this assignment immediate
contact was made with the named insured and a subsequent
appointment to meet with the Whiten family was arranged the same
afternoon at 3:00 p.m.

     On the above date and time, I attended at Haliburton and met
with the insureds who were staying with friends Rex and Elsie
Massey who reside on County Road #1 just south of Haliburton.

     Attached to this report is a transcribed copy of the dictated
statement secured from Keith Whiten with assistance from his wife
Daphne and their daughter Louise.

156

EX. 15

InterSpect
National Claims Service

FRANCIS, LABRASH, QUIBELL & ASSOCIATES
INSURANCE ADJUSTERS INC.
Bobcaygeon   P.O. Box 972
            Bobcaygeon, Ont. K0M 1A0
            Tel (705) 738-5141   Fax: (705) 738-5142

YOUR FILE   94L0410
OUR FILE   1505-B

February 25, 1994

PILOT INSURANCE COMPANY
90 Eglington Ave.,
Toronto, Ontario
M4P 1E9

CERTIFIED TO BE A TRUE AND CORREC
COPY OF THE ORIGINAL GIVEN UNDER
MY HAND AND THE SEAL OF THIS COUR
COPIE AUTHENTIQUE CERTIFIÉE ET
CONFORME À L'ORIGINAL
EN FOI DE QUOI, J'AI SIGNE ET APPOSI
LE SCEAU DE CETTE COUR

ATTN: Chris Porter

CC: Steve Carter

THIS ___ DAY O___ ___ 2004

FAIT LE _____ 20 ___

RE - INSURED: Keith Whiten & Daphne Whiten
DATE OF LOSS: January 18, 1994

FOR REGISTRAR / GREFFIER
COURT OF APPEAL FOR ONTARIO
COUR D'APPEL DE L'ONTARIO

Dear Sir,

Further to my report of February 3, 1994 and our subsequent telephone conversations with Mr Carter, as instructed I have asked the insured's solicitor Donald Finn to confirm in writing the arrangements he had made for a new mortgage for the Whitens. Upon receipt of Mr Finn's letter, it will be sent to you with my comments.

With respects to the I.C.P.B., on Mr Carter's instructions we requested their indulgence in this investigation. After receiving the assignment, Gary South of the I.C.P.B. in Orillia contacted the writer and the circumstances were reviewed in detail. When Mr South learned that our own engineer had been involved and had determined the probable cause of the fire, he declined any further involvement stating that #1 - we did have a possible motive, #2 - there was opportunity but #3 - if we came into court with the engineering evidence and this probable cause, we wouldn't have a leg to stand on as far as declining the claim.

Mr South will provide me with a letter to this effect and when it is received by my office, it will be passed along to you.

As outlined in my 2nd report with the physical evidence we have and the fact that the insured was attempting to arrange financing through another source and pay off the existing mortgage, there is little or no base to deny this claim. I certainly agree with your train of thought and if we did not have the physical evidence and the information from the insured's solicitor that he was arranging financing for the Whitens, then my recommendations would certainly be opposite to what they are today. Unfortunately we must deal with the facts on hand and proceed with the adjustment accordingly in my opinion.

InterSpect

502
Derek Francis, in-chf (Will)
Monday, November 20, 1995

BY MR. WILL:

    Q. All right. So the January 18, '94, is your handwriting?

    A. Yes, it is, and this here is my handwriting.

    Q. All right. And the second page of this preliminary claim notice.

    A. Mm-hmm.

    Q. Is this a copy of a document that you would have prepared?

    A. This is -- this is taken from the information contained on here except they omit those items there, and they proceed and this is sent in to the insurance company for acknowledgement of the assignment.

    Q. Who prepared this document?

    A. My secretary.

    Q. And that was sent to Pilot Insurance on January 19th?

    A. Yes, with a copy to Pilot Insurance Company in Toronto.

    Q. All right. Who were you reporting to at Pilot Insurance in Toronto?

    A. It just goes to their head office, and then they designate the file. In this case, it turned out to be a fellow by the name of Chris Porter.

    Q. All right. And who were you reporting to at Pilot Insurance in Peterborough?

    A. Steve Carter.

    THE COURT: Steve?

548
Derek Francis, in-chf (Will)
Wednesday, November 22, 1995

Q. Okay. And Keith Whiten told you about that?

A. Yes, he did.

Q. And I take it this information was obtained by you in response to questions that were asked of you -- by you -- sorry.

A. Yes.

Q. And all the questions that you asked regarding their financial circumstances were answered by Keith and Daphne Whiten?

A. Yes, they were.

Q. All right. Now, you still have your February 3rd, 1994, report?

A. Yes, I do.

Q. Could you turn to page 2 of that report?

A. Mm-hmm.

Q. At the top of that -- now, this is a report that you sent to Chris Porter at Pilot Insurance?

A. Yes, and to Steven Carter at Pilot in Peterborough.

Q. And do you know that the report was received by each of them?

A. I expect it was.

Q. Did you discuss this report, the contents of this report, with Steve Carter and Chris Porter?

A. The contents of the report, in part, were discussed with Steve Carter.

Q. All right. And did you discuss this report of February 3rd, 1994, with anyone other than Steve Carter?

594
Derek Francis, in-chf (Will)
Wednesday, November 22, 1995

you to proceed.

BY MR. WILL:

Q. Mr. Francis, do you report in this letter to Pilot Insurance of February 25th that Gary South of the Insurance Crime Prevention Bureau told you that:

> "If we came into court with the engineering evidence and this probable cause, we wouldn't have a leg to stand on as far as declining the claim."

A. That is correct.

Q. That's what Gary South told you?

A. Yes.

Q. And you told Pilot Insurance?

A. And I reported that to Pilot, yes.

Q. And Mr. South also told you in that conversation that he would give you a letter to this effect?

A. Yes, he did.

Q. And you indicate in your report that you would pass that letter on to Pilot Insurance?

A. Yes, I did.

Q. Now, in the next paragraph of your report, you start the paragraph by saying: "As outlined in my second report," and --

A. Yes. That's the report of February 3rd.

Q. All right. Now, is that the second report that you --

595
Derek Francis, in-chf (Will)
Wednesday, November 22, 1995

    A. Yes.

    Q. -- prepared for Pilot Insurance --

    A. Yes, it is.

    Q. All right. And where is the first report
that you --

    A. The first report is the preliminary report.

    Q. That was that one-page document?

    A. Yes.

    Q. And there was no other report sent to Pilot
between that preliminary report and the report of February
3rd?

    A. No.

    Q. All right. You say in this report:

"As outlined in my second report, with the
physical evidence we have and the fact that the
insured was attempting to arrange financing
through another source and pay off the existing
mortgage, there is little or no base to deny
this claim."

    A. That's correct.

    Q. That was your opinion?

    A. Yes, it was.

    Q. And the next sentence says that: "I
certainly agree with your train of thought." Now, whose train
of thought are you referring to there?

    A. This would probably be to -- referring to
Mr. Carter's train of thought.

596
Derek Francis, in-chf (Will)
Wednesday, November 22, 1995

Q. So it was Mr. Carter as opposed to
Mr. Porter?

A. Yes.

Q. All right. Well, what did you mean by
that: "I certainly agree with your train of thought." What
was the train of thought that was being conveyed to you by
Steve Carter?

A. I think there was a -- there was a train of
thought that there was poor financial -- a poor financial
situation, and that led to thoughts of other -- other than
being accidental. You know, that's what I got from the
conversation.

Q. All right. Well, so as of February 25 of
1994, did Steve Carter tell you that he thought this was an
arson?

A. No, he never said that he thought it was an
arson.

Q. Well, so by your statement: "I certainly
agree with your train of thought," you were just referring to
the --

A. Well, you have got a situation where you
have got total loss file. You have got a poor financial
situation, and that does rise to give some suspicion, and that
was the train of thought: Is this a suspicious fire?

Q. So Steve Carter thought this was a
suspicious fire on February 25, 1994?

A. I'm not certain. I can't answer for Steve
Carter.

Q. Well --

770
Derek Francis, re-ex (Will)
Thursday, November 23, 1995

Q. Now, Mr. Francis, we were speaking about when you learnt about the bankruptcy of Keith Whiten. You were advised by Pilot?

A. I was advised by Pilot.

Q. Do you know how you were advised? Was it by telephone?

A. Either by telephone or by discussion with Steve Carter.

Q. All right. And do you believe it was Steve Carter that told you that as opposed to anyone else?

A. Yes.

Q. And do you have a recollection of what month that discussion took place?

A. Late February, March, mid-March.

Q. And would you agree with me that you then had the information with respect to the bankruptcy prior to your April 28th report to Mr. Crabbe?

A. If that's correct, yes. I can't say it's a hundred percent correct, because I don't have my file.

Q. And you'll be able to confirm that once you get your complete file?

A. I hope so, yes.

Q. Now, would you confirm for me that you had Hugh Carter's report of March 25th, 1994?

A. Again, my same answer with respects I don't have my file; I can't confirm whether I have got it or I haven't got it.

Q. Do you have a copy of this report with you now?

1238
Tuesday, November 28, 1995

MR. WILL: (Reading)

"QUESTION 37: Okay. Do you know whether Pilot
Insurance Company is owned -- do
you know exactly who owns Pilot
Insurance Company? Is it
General Accident or a subsidiary
of General Accident or do you
know?

ANSWER: As far as I know, General
Accident."

Page 9:
"QUESTION 41: Thank you. Now, can you tell
me, Mr. Carter, to whom you
report at head office in a
claims-related matter when
there's been a loss?

ANSWER: Most instances George Hamilton."

Page 10
"QUESTION 49: Okay. What's the monetary value
of the claims that get reported
to the head office?

ANSWER: Excess of $60,000.

QUESTION 51: All right. Now, what is
Mr. Hamilton's title at head
office?

ANSWER: Assistant to the vice president.

QUESTION: Okay. Do you know if he is the

1348.
Wednesday, November 29, 1995

discovery that he's really got a hand in things that you didn't think of earlier -- that you didn't think he had earlier. I know that he was aware of this matter. I know he was being consulted about it, and I'm presuming he was also a participant in the decision to deny the claim.

QUESTION: Well, would you ask that question, please, who it was that made that decision.

MR. CRABBE: Yes."

MR. WILL: And in answer to the undertaking, the answer given was by letter dated October 4th, 1995. The ultimate decision to deny the claim was Mr. Jones.

"QUESTION 505: Other than the Retrac reports and associated reports and the reports and investigation by Origin and Cause, Mr. Francis, Mr. Couch and the Loumar report of February 24th, 1994, what, if any, investigation has Pilot every taken in relation to this matter?

"MR. CRABBE: There was also some in-house

"the above quotes from the evidence before the Supreme Court is a replica and not represented as an official version of the evidence which was certified by the Court of Appeal for Ontario"

CHAPTER TWELVE

<u>Rules of Law That Did Not Protect My Name</u>

"Since the Charter protects individuals and minority groups from laws and government actions that violate their constitutional rights, it does not apply to civil actions where there is no state involvement. The Supreme Court of Canada, however, has ruled that the civil law should reflect the values of fairness and justice enshrined in the Charter.

The common law has the potential to produce rulings that may be unfair or unjust. Judges apply a set of rules known as the principles of equity to ensure no one with a worthy case will fall through the cracks of the justice system. One equitable principle holds that there must be a legal remedy for every wrong. Another demand that litigants come to court with clean hands—the courts will not readily side with a person who has failed to act honourably or has tried to take advantage of someone else. The concept of a trust flows from the law of equity, ensuring that a dominant party does not profit at the expense of a weaker one.

The Charter of Rights and Freedoms came into force in 1982. Section s. 52 (1) of the Constitution Act, 1982, declares that the constitution, which includes the Charter, is "the supreme law of Canada, and any law that is inconsistent with the provisions of the Constitution is, to the extent of the inconsistency, of no force and effect."

The Supreme Court of Canada has described the judge as "the pillar of our entire justice system." The judge has many roles. In the words of the Greek philosopher Socrates: "Four things belong to a judge: to hear courteously, to answer wisely, to consider soberly, and to decide impartially." The judge oversees the proceedings, keeping order in the courtroom and ensuring the case runs smoothly. Sometimes the judge takes on the role of an umpire, resolving disputes that arise over the law and how a case should proceed. The judge decides whether evidence is relevant to the issues before the court and, if it is not, will prevent it from being used.

The province of Quebec has had its share of dictatorship going back to the Duplessis Government and whereas Quebec is under the Civil Code, the Charter applies to individual rights under the Criminal Code of Canada. Individual basic rights from Quebec to British Columbia are: i. a right to a jury trial; ii. Right to be given proper notice; iii. Providing full disclosure; iv. Right of cross-examination; v. Right to face his accuse; vi. Right to counsel; right to be tried in an open court; vii. Right to be tried by an unbiased decision-maker; viii. Habeas corpus;"

The above material was taken from resource material entitled 'Why do we need Judges?' This is on the Ministry of Justice for Canada website at the following Internet address: http://www.tryjudging.ca/downloads/english/pdf/students/YBTJ_module01.pdf

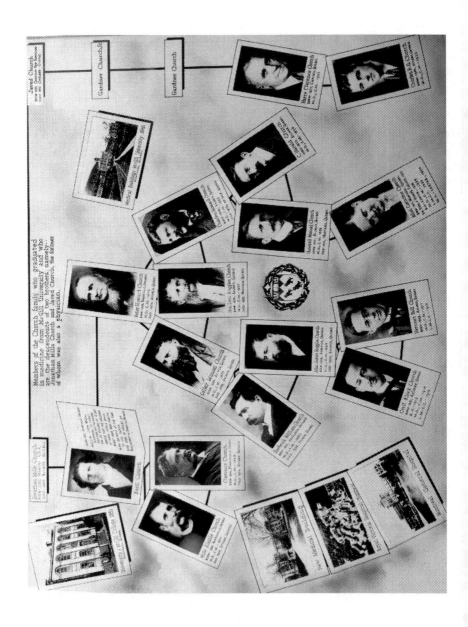

PART TWO

THE FUSION OF HISTORICITY
AND NATURAL JUSTICE?

CHAPTER THIRTEEN

Disrespect for a Private Citizen of Canada

The challenge of this case and the fact that there was no one to assist in the investigation of a Supreme Court of Canada mistake has been enlightening to both me and my wife in the profession we now practice as private investigators.

The mistake was made in its findings which I believe were made without proper support. However the Supreme Court of Canada also used references to me like Rogue, Delinquent etc., and used my name in reference to the train of thought at Pilot Insurance Company with regard to the denial of the Whitens' fire claim. It is difficult to contest a Supreme Court of Canada judgment after it has been rendered, if not impossible. Therefore the question I felt was, how to react? I thought about how another family member would feel about our family name being tarnished with such defamatory references.

Perhaps one would wonder how my 3rd great grandmother of would have felt about her descendent being called names by a Supreme Court of Canada judge without an opportunity to speak and defend himself. Mary Ann Hayden Church, wife of Dr. Basil Rorison Church, "is believed to be the first female preacher to form a congregation in Canada",[1] with the Unitary Church of Canada. Mary Church might have preached the 9th Commandment to the Justice of the Supreme Court of Canada.

---

[1] Heather Fraser Fawcett, Invisible Influence Unitarian women—Canada-History March 2011

Dr. Basil Rorison Church was a member of the Legislative Assembly of the Province of Canada and was also the uncle of Hon. Levi Ruggles Church. However he was also my 3rd great-grandfather and therefore although the name Church cannot be found in the name Porter, what is inherited is the ancestral connection of the person and the name is a part of the very being of Chris Porter.

It is out of respect and admiration for the members of the ancestors who make up my family, that makes the following an example of the damage caused by the disrespect shown by the Supreme Court of Canada for a private citizen of Canada. Disrespect for the name and disrespect for the law.

CHAPTER FOURTEEN

Ancestral Historicity

"Levi Ruggles Church, Q.C., Montreal, was born at Aylmer, on May 26, 1836. He is descended from one of the oldest families in New England, his ancestors having immigrated from the old country to the colony of Massachusetts, in the early part of the seventeenth century. One of these, Colonel Benjamine Church, distinguished himself in the French and Indian Wars in which the New England colonists were engaged, having commanded the volunteer army, which in a protracted kind of guerrilla warfare, defeated and afterwards, killed the celebrated Indian King Philip, who had given so much trouble and alarm to the early settlers.

The Benjamin Church Plaque is owned by the Rhode
Island Society of Colonial Wars

At the breaking out of the revolutionary war, the Church family,
respectable both in numbers and position, being Whigs, espoused
the Republican cause, except two, who took up arms to defend the
Royal prerogative. One of these was killed in battle, and the other,
Jonathan Mills Church, (4th great-grandfather of Chris Porter), was
taken prisoner in 1777, by the American Army, from whose custody
he escaped and came to Canada, and ultimately settled in Brockville,
Ontario. He took an active part in defending Canada during the war
of 1812-13-14, and died at a very advanced age in 1846.

The subject is the second son of the late Dr. Peter Howard Church
of Aylmer, P.Q. Dr. Peter Howard Church was the brother of Dr.
Basil Rorison Church, and son of Jonathan Mills Church. The
second son of Dr. Peter Howard Church was Levi Ruggles Church
and he was educated at Victoria University, Cobourg, Ontario.
He graduated in Medicine at the Albany Medical College, and
at McGill University, where he took his final and primary thesis
prizes. He studied law under the late Henry Stuart, Q.C., and
subsequently under Edward Carter, Q.C., and was called to the
bar, Lower Canada, in 1859. He was created a Q.C., in 1874. He
sat for the County of Ottawa from 1867 to 1871, when he retired,
but on accepting office in 1874, was returned by acclamation for
the County of Pontiac, and was re-elected by acclamation at the
general election of 1876, and again in 1880, after a contest.

He was a member of the law firm of Church, Chapleau, Hall
& Nicholls, Montreal, P.Q. At the formation of the Chapleau
administration in 1883, he was offered the treasure ship of the
Province, which he again declined, preferring the active practice
of his profession. He married on September 3rd 1850, Jane Erskine
Bell, daughter of William Bell, barrister, and niece of General
Sir George Bell, K.C.B. The importance of raising the name
Levi Ruggles Church, was to point out the relevance of a family
member in a role similar to that of the Chief Justice. Levi Ruggles
Church was one of the founding fathers of a law firm that became

known as Ogilvy Renault. He was a Conservative member of the Quebec Legislative Assembly as mentioned for the County of Ottawa and also became a crown attorney for the Ottawa District. He spent his final years as a judge on the Court of the Queen's Bench from October 25, 1887 until January 7, 1892. He is buried beside his wife, father and Jonathan Mills Church, his grandfather in Aylmer, P.Q. His name was respected throughout his entire life and to this day is honoured for his contribution to Quebec and the legal community including Ogilvy Renault who honour his name on their website.

Included in these historical accounts is a rather unique history of the Church family remaining as the sole medical doctors for Aylmer, P.Q. for 127 years providing medical services for Aylmer and the Ottawa community and that Dr. Clarence Church with the help of a certain member of the Royal family was able to start a hospital in Ottawa called St. Luke's that amalgamated with what is now called the Ottawa Civic Hospital. Dr. Clarence Roland Church is the cousin of Judge Levi Ruggles Church Q.C., of Montreal born in Merrickville, Ontario September 26, 1846 and is the son of Dr. Basil Rorison Church, U.E.L." 5

They had another cousin residing near Albany New York, by the name of Frederic Edwin Church, a famous landscape artist, who studied under Thomas Cole. Among the many paintings which are displayed in Hartford at the Wadsworth Athenaeum, is a painting by Frederic Edwin Church called "The Hooker Party Migrated to Hartford". This painting depicts the ancestors of Frederic Edwin Church as well as the ancestors of Levi Ruggles Church, and Chris Porter, wandering in the wilderness to find and discover Hartford, Connecticut. Richard Church is displayed with his wife Anne Marsh, with a horse and the Reverend Hooker party. What this painting also displays is the struggle and courage is must have taken in the 17th century to bring a family from Europe to the North America.

Perhaps the Supreme Court should have examined the person they were condemning before passing sentence on his name and reputation, a reputation which can be traced back to the very beginnings of civilization in North America. Richard Church is my 9th great-grandfather and was identified by the United States of America Government as one of the founding fathers of Hartford, Connecticut and also discovered and founded Hadley, Hampshire Massachusetts U.S.A. His descendent Frederic Edwin Church is buried along with his family members in Hartford, Connecticut.

There are other family names which can be traced to the name Chris Porter. Many of my ancestors played a significant role in the development of Canada and the freedom we enjoy as citizens of this great country. The importance of raising their names and describing what is recorded in history about who they were is meant to convey the importance of how we are described by those who come after, from accounts such as described by the Supreme Court of Canada ruling where they have forevermore contaminated and destroyed my reputation and those who's names I carry.

In the Municipal Election of 2000, I began to listen to my heart and desire to run for office. However even though I lost in my bid to become a member of the local Government, my taste for representing the citizens of my local constituency had begun to take hold. This all came to an end in 2002 when the Supreme Court announced to the world a fabricated relationship between my name and the train of thought that lead to the largest award for punitive damages in Canadian history.

Dr. Basil Rorison Church had a granddaughter by the name, Mildred Gwendolyn Church, daughter of Dr. Clarence Ronald Church, who was the wife of the grandson of Sir Casimir Stanislaus Gzowski, who was named Casimir Stanislaus Gzowski. The Supreme Court would have you believe that a surname has no real meaning or purpose. However if Sir Casimir Stanislaus Gzowski not been at one time the aide-de-camp to Queen Victoria, the Queen's Plate might not have come to Canada which was among many important achievements attained for Canada by Sir Casimir Stanislaus Gzowski.

"Miss Mary Gzowski of Montreal graciously enabled the authors of a book entitled Sir Casimir Stanislaus Gzowski A Biography, to examine the documents in her possession concerning the Gzowski family. Among these is a photostat copy of a certified copy of resolution of the nobility deputation of the Grodno government dated October 11, 1817, and stating that the Gzowski family belonged to the Polish nobility. Grodno was within the boundaries of the Grand Duchy of Lithuania, the latter forming a part of the Polish Commonwealth, hence the adjective "Lithuania".

The history of the noble family of Gzowski bearing the Junosza coat of arms. On the 11th day of October in the year of 1817." In this same book it is stated that, "Sir Casimir Gzowski's work has been rewarded by the government of Ontario by a bronze statue described in the report of the park superintendent for the year 1891 as follows: "Early in the summer a most valuable and highly acceptable gift was made to the Park by the Government of Ontario. In recognition of the services so freely rendered the Province, for so many years, by the Park Commissioners, a beautiful bronze statute of the Chairman, Sir Casimir Gzowski, was erected in the Park and unveiled on the 25th July. The brass plate inscription reads: Colonel Sir Casimir Gzowski K.C.M.G., Aide de Camp to the Queen, Chairman of the Queen Victoria Niagara Falls Park Commission."

Dr. Clarence Ronald Church is my 2nd great-grandfather. In 1896 he was recognized for his professional standing and merit being elected President of the Ottawa Branch of the British Medical Association. He took a marked interest in Freemasonry and remained in close affiliation with his mother lodge until the last. Otherwise, he had reached the highest rung in the ladder of the Order, for he was a member of the Scottish Rite and Knight Templar, holding office as such under H.R.H. The Prince of Wales.

Perhaps, the most distinguishing feature of Dr. Church's character was his sturdy spirit of loyalty. Having had an ancestor who had served and who had fallen with Lord Nelson, at Trafalgar. His love of everything British, when ever he went to England, he visited the Victory, and kissed the spot, hallowed by the blood of our great hero. He died on April 20, 1900 in his home in Aylmer, P.Q., and his remains were carried by buggy and horseback to Merrickville, Ontario where he is buried beside his father Basil Rorison Church, mother Mary Ann (Haydon) Church, his wife Marguerite Elizabeth (LaRue) Church and his daughter Maude Louise (Church) Hamilton.

Maude Louise (Church) Hamilton is my great-grandmother and died at the age of 41 from tuberculosis. She was the wife of another great-grandfather of mine by the name of Lt. Col. Andrew Lorne Hamilton. He had been a Colonel in World War One and the Secretary-Treasurer of the Last Post Fund, a fund established to assist in the burial of soldiers who had made the ultimate sacrifice. Lt. Col. Andrew Lorne Hamilton was awarded the C.M.G. by King George V for his efforts and sacrifice during World War One.

The Central Chancery of the Orders of Knighthood, St. James Palace, has recorded that the citation published in the London Gazette at the time of his award read as follows:

"The King has been graciously pleased, on the occasion of His Majesty's Birthday, to give directions for the following promotions in, and appointments to, the Most Distinguished Order of Saint Michael and Saint George, for services rendered in connection with the Military Operations in France and Flanders. Dated 3rd June, 1918:—To be Additional Members of the Third Class, or Companions, of the said Most Distinguished Order:—Canadian Forces, Maj. (T./Lt.-Col.) Andrew Lorne Hamilton, Can. A.P.C."

In a newspaper in Canada after the announcement of his death, it was recorded that; it was widely believed that Lt. Col. Andrew

Lorne Hamilton, might have been Knighted had it not been outlawed in Canada. Lt. Col. Andrew Lorne Hamilton served in World War 1 as Colonel and Assistant Adjutant General with the Canadian Section General Headquarters, Third Echelon, in France. Later he was director of records overseas for the military forces of Canada at London. He was mentioned in dispatches three times. A member of the non-permanent active militia, he enlisted at the outbreak of the war with the 8th Regiment, Royal Rifles. In 1943 he was appointed treasurer of the Last Post Fund, and was prominent in the Masonic Order.

BUCKINGHAM PALACE

The Defence Services Secretary is
Commanded by Her Majesty The Queen to
acknowledge the receipt of Mr
Porter's letter which has been
referred to the Ministry of Defence.

26th February 1998

CENTRAL CHANCERY OF THE ORDERS OF KNIGHTHOOD
ST JAMES'S PALACE, SW1A 1BH
TELEPHONE · 0171-930 4832
FAX · 0171-839 2983
From: Lieutenant Colonel Anthony Mather, CVO, OBE

Reference: 26/4/98   5th March 1998

Dear Mr Porter

Thank you for your letter of 13th February concerning Lieutenant Colonel Andrew L. Hamilton.

From our records held here in the Central Chancery, we have found that Lieutenant Colonel Hamilton was awarded the CMG (Additional Companion of the Most Distinguished Order of St. Michael and St. George) on 3rd June 1918. The citation published in the London Gazette at the time of his award read as follows

"The King has been graciously pleased, on the occasion of His Majesty's Birthday, to give directions for the following promotions in, and appointments to, the Most Distinguished Order of Saint Michael and Saint George, for services rendered in connection with the Military Operations in France and Flanders. Dated 3rd June, 1918:-

To be Additional Members of the Third Class, or Companions, of the said Most Distinguished Order:-

Canadian Force

Maj. (T./Lt.-Col.) Andrew Lorne Hamilton, Can. A.P.C."

I hope this information will be of assistance.

Yours sincerely,

Deputy Secretary,
The Order of St. Michael and St. George

Chris Porter Esq.,

cc. Secretary to the Defence Services Secretary

It is with a great deal of pride and enjoyment that I record the genealogical research I have collected on members of my ancestral family. However, clearly this account is recorded in an effort to assist the reader of this book, to understand how I believe the damage to me may have affected the reputation of my entire family. The account by the Supreme Court of Canada of who I was and my role at Pilot Insurance Company is simply a fabrication of the truth and without any merit.

My grandmother, Helena Maude (Hamilton) de Camps and daughter of Andrew Lorne Hamilton and Maude Louise (Church) Hamilton, became the wife of yet another person of relevance namely my grandfather, Edward Beaconsfield Edgar de Camps. He respected the name Beaconsfield because of the reference it made to another great person of relevance in England called Benjamin Disraeli, Prime Minister of Great Britain, who received that name from Queen Victoria, when her Majesty bestowed upon him the name Lord Beaconsfield. Edward de Camps was from Cowbit, England however his ancestors fled France because they were Presbyterian and therefore called Huguenot by the French Government. His ancestors came to Cowbit, Spalding England and became citizens of England and adopted the English culture. In 1905 Edward de Camps left from Cobalt England and came to Canada attracted by a certain gold rush in Nova Scotia and then to Ontario where he opened the first copper minds in Canada. He had a very close friendship with Sir Winston Churchill and was quoted in many newspapers for his expertise on minerals and metals that would affect the stock market and the U.S. Military used his expertise on magnesium during world war two.

Edward de Camps came to Canada with two items of interest to him, one was a book of photographs taken by Queen Alexandra, a book only given as a Christmas gift to close friends and relatives and perhaps the second is only folklore. Edward de Camps talked about a special ring he came to Canada with that was once owned by Flora MacDonald a gift possibly from a certain Prince Charlie? Apparently this ring Edward lost while mining in Hailbury, Ontario. Stories of fact and fiction creep into the fabric of our history and sometimes they come from within the family and sometimes they are described by others who may or may not have accurate honest accounts of family members. However when a person is still living and able to answer questions why would not those who want to label that person, not simply ask for a response to the allegation before making the allegation, knowing how damaging it would be for that individual. Clearly no act of fairness was considered by the Supreme Court of Canada and no rights were allowed before sentencing.

One of the last members of my ancestral family with which I account for is a great-aunt by the name of Mildred Church Hamilton, the daughter of Col. Andrew Lorne Hamilton and sister of my grandmother, Helena Maude Hamilton. Mildred assembled most of the family tree information I account for in this book, while she was working for the Right Honourable Charles Vincent Massey, 18th Governor General of Canada, during World War Two at Canada House in London, England. Working as his secretary during that time must have been difficult given the role Canada had in Europe and the fact that Canada House played an important role with the war effort. It is likely that her position and responsibilities were extended to say the least. It was Mildred's (Mimi's) heart and commitment to the family and our ancestors that allowed me to receive a copy of her family tree after her death. However I have always had a great deal of respect for a woman (great-aunt), being to me a real war hero.

Mildred Church Hamilton was the great-granddaughter of Dr. James C. Hamilton who was my 3rd great-grandfather. This was yet another ancestor connected to Chris Porter who carried a great deal of respect both in the United States of America, Scotland and Canada. Dr. Hamilton was born in the village of Douglas, Lanarkshire, Scotland in 1797. He died on March 1, 1877 in West Flamborough, Ontario. He graduated in Medicine at the Royal College of Surgeons and attended the University of Edinborough in Scotland. He was involved in the creation of the Welland Canal, the Wellington Grey and Bruce Railway as well as the Great Western Railway. He held a commission as Lieutenant-Colonel of the 3rd Regiment of the Halton Militia, and was involved in active service. He took part in the suppression of the rebellion of 1837 and was with the Loyalists in their siege of Navy Island. A respected member of his profession, Dr. Hamilton was appointed to the Upper Canada Medical Board in 1836 and represented Burlington and the home district on the Ontario Medical Council from 1869 until 1872.

In private life Dr. James C. Hamilton married Anne Draper Hatt who is my 3rd great-grandmother. There is an ancestral connection with Chris Porter and Camilla Parker Bowles, Duchess of Cornwall, revealed in November 2009 when the Duchess visited Dundurn Castle. Sophia Mary MacNab, daughter of Sir Allan Napier MacNab is the 3rd great-grandmother of Camilla Parker Bowles and Sophia is the niece of Lucy Eloise MacNab 3rd great-grand-aunt-in-law and spouse of Chris Porter's 3rd great-uncle, John Olgilvie Hatt who is the grandson of Richard Hatt the 4th great-grandfather of Chris Porter and who was recently acknowledged as the founding father of Dundas, Ontario. Anne Draper Hatt is the daughter of Richard Hatt and sister of John Olgilvie Hatt. Dr. James C. Hamilton had a very close friendship with Sir Allan Napier MacNab and there was a significant beginning to the start of Sir Allan Napier MacNab's Political Life and that of his Tory party which began at 'Spring Hill' the home of Dr. Hamilton which looked over Dundas, Ontario from West Flamborough, Ontario.

CHAPTER FIFTEEN

<u>Family Names</u>

Clearly if there is any intrinsic significance in a family name and those who were the future descendents of those family names than there is indeed a significant concern raised by the fabricated use of one of those names by the Supreme Court of Canada. If there was a negative rippling effect recorded in history without any acknowledgement or challenge by me or the recipient of the transgression affecting the name of my family, then it could be simply stated as described by the Supreme Court Judge, that Chris Porter was a rogue examiner at Pilot Insurance Company who promoted a train of thought that was the catalyst in what drove Pilot Insurance Company to commit the atrocity for which Pilot Insurance Company was condemned by his Supreme Court of Canada. This of course is all based on no testimony from Chris Porter, no accusations by the plaintiff in the case and no desire on the part of anybody except the Supreme Court Judge to damage my family name.

This account is my attempt to demonstrate how a surname carries forward the historical efforts of generations of families that came before us. The struggle and efforts by historical family members was and is always a desire for our future generations to exist with the dignity and opportunity life has to offer. Take for instance my name also carries the name Guy which was given to me by my grandfather who's son Guy Cyr de Camps died at the age of 6 from scarlet fever. My name Chris Porter was given to me by my mother and father Dr. Charles Jack Porter. How did the

Supreme Court of Canada not damage his name when calling me names when releasing their findings in Whiten v. Pilot Insurance Company without proper support?

Dr. Porter not only worked all his life for his family but also contributed significantly to our entire society. Dr. Charles Jack Porter, known to all of us as Jack, and a pioneer of clinical chemistry in Canada and Founding Member of our society passed away in October 2006.

"Dr. Porter was born in Royal Oak, Oakland, Michigan, USA and grew up in Port Arthur, Ontario. He received his B.A. in Chemistry at McMaster University in 1944. He worked for 2 years at Connaught Medical Research Laboratories and for 2 years as an analytical chemist at British Drug Houses in Toronto. He met and married his wife, Dorothy, in 1948, and then embarked on his Ph.D. in Biochemistry at the University of Toronto, which he obtained in 1953. He then worked as a research biochemist at Merck in Montreal. He was recruited by Dr. Murray Young in 1957 to be head of the Division of Chemistry and Biochemistry (later Biochemist-in-Chief), Toronto General Hospital, until his retirement in 1984. He was an Associate Professor in the Department of Pathological Chemistry at the University of Toronto.

He was a Founding member of the Hospitals In Common Laboratory in Toronto in 1969, and served as a director on its Board of Governors. After retirement, he continued his involvement as a director until 2002, when he was in his 80s.

His society memberships included Ontario Society of Clinical Chemists, Canadian Biochemical Society (Founding Member), American Association for Clinical Chemistry, Academy of Clinical Laboratory Physicians and Scientists.

Dr. Porter was always deeply involved in education and in professional society activity. At Toronto General Hospital, he was Program Director of the Post-doctoral Diploma and Medical

Biochemistry Training Programs, and Director of the Medical Laboratory Technology Training Program. He served on both the Executive Committee and Advisory Council of the Michener Institute for Applied Health Technology (formerly Toronto Institute of Medical Technology).

Within the Canadian Society of Clinical Chemists, he was a Founding Member (1956), and received his CSCC certification in 1965. He served on numerous Committees: Certification, Instrumentation, Quality Control, Education, and Reference and Reference Methods. He served as Vice—President (1964-65), and President (1966). He was also a member of the Central Coordinating Committee for the IX International Congress on Clinical Chemistry, Toronto in 1975, and chaired the Scientific Program. Dr. Porter received the Ames Award for Outstanding Contributions to Clinical Chemistry from the CSCC in 1971.

He was also concerned with education at the international level, serving as member and secretary of the Education Committee of the International Federation of Clinical Chemistry (IFCC), and member and secretary of Commission on Teaching of Clinical Chemistry of the International Union of Pure and Applied Chemistry (IUPAC). He was able to combine his interests in clinical chemistry, education and travel by reportedly attending every IFCC meeting as far back as 1972, and perhaps even earlier. He made many friends among his colleagues in the clinical chemistry community in Canada and throughout the world."— Obituary CSCC News, By, Dr. Lynn C. Allen, Department of Clinical Biochemistry, ES 3-404, The Toronto Hospital, General Division, 200 Elizabeth Street, Toronto, Ontario M5G, 2C4, Canada.

The last person I will mention who is passed away, is my mother, Dorothy Mildred (de Camps) Porter. My memories of my mother in Montreal when I was growing up are of my mother, with my brothers, waiting for my father in a winter storm, at the Beaconsfield train station, at the end of Angell Avenue where we lived. We would be standing in the snow just waiting for his return from work. She was a dedicated person who sacrificed to raise a family and support her husband and children. Towards the end of her life my ability to assist her had been affected by the damage caused to me by this case. In one of the last vacations my mother and I ever had together with my father was to visit Montreal and Quebec City and of course visit a favorite place to both of us known as Sainte-Anne-de-Beaupré.

We are not responsible for the naming of ourselves and we actually inherit the very name we carry. It is an honour and one which should not with such flagrant abuse by the justices of the Supreme Court of Canada be tarnished and utilized for corporate benefit or any other benefit for which it was not intended. The use of a name is sacred and should be treated with respect not disrespect. Therefore when the Supreme Court of Canada shows such flagrant disregard and disrespect, contrary to our natural laws and contrary to the very law which is enacted by the Parliament of Canada, does this not diminish their role, status and supremacy? Perhaps the Government of Canada should reverse this abuse and bring forth legislation which would reverse this decision and prevent future acts by the Supreme Court of Canada or any other court in this Country from abusing the natural rights entailed by a person's name.

There is no doubt that the current Prime Minister of Canada who was officially informed on behalf of Chris Porter by his Member of Parliament about the abomination in the reference to Chris Porter in this ruling, that the Prime Minister would not be disturbed by what has transpired.

The Ministry of Justice reviewed the manuscript for this book for nine weeks in 2009 and was not able to provide any reaction as stated by the Minister of Justice and Attorney General of Canada. Clearly, the Supreme Court of Canada has committed a transgression for which they refuse to correct. The Supreme Court of Canada act for the Government of Canada along with the

Ministry of Justice and therefore how could it be expected that the Prime Minister, as understanding as he might be, be expected to interfere and intervene. It is clearly a dilemma that he could not be expected to resolve. However it is my hope at least that he is aware of what has transpired in my life and how this judgment has curtailed what would have otherwise been a more meaningful, fulfilling and fruitful life. Perhaps we need to add the words, "We the People" to the first sentence of our Constitution or Charter of Rights.

PART THREE

MORAL INDIFFERENCE

CHAPTER SIXTEEN

Canadian Law With Respect to The Law of Rights & Liberties

Chief Justice of the Supreme Court of Canada, April 5, 2005 Speech on Democracy

Comparative View of the United States and Canada Protecting Constitutional Rights

The Following is a Paraphrase Summary from Excerpts from the Speech as Required by the Supreme Court of Canada

The Chief Justice of the Supreme Court of Canada gave a speech on April 5, 2005 that was of particular interest to me because the speech provided us with a window into her understanding of Canadian law with respect to the law of rights and liberties. These laws reflect in her words fundamental social and moral assumptions that reflected the national character of Canada. The speech went on to compare Canada and the United States and the difference in public discourse that emerged from the very different history and the effects of how each country attained independence. The United States rejected its colonial authority whereas Canada evolved by embracing its European colonial past.

The American Constitution begins with the words "We the People" whereas the words are absent from the Canadian Constitution. She expresses the view that the Provinces had a desire to be federally united to the one Dominion. In her speech she is discussing all the examples of freedoms and how they are perceived differently by each nation. With the one hundred years it took to adopt the bill of rights in Canada it is the belief of the Chief Justice that we are comfortable with the Charter of Rights and Freedoms and in her words because it begins with the acknowledgement of the state's right to limit basic rights and freedoms. Americans on the other hand had to abruptly reject its colonial past with bloody revolution and rejection of the past to protect individual citizen against the tyranny of the state. In the view of the Chief Justice that is why Canadians trust the state and Americans are less willing to trust the state and will blame the state for poverty and medical needs that are not met. This explains why there is a difference in both societies about individual rights and why groups as a whole achieve a different process and discourse.

What the Chief Justice is basically saying is that the Charter of Rights and Freedoms as interpreted by the Supreme Court of Canada, begins with an acknowledgement or proclamation that the state's right exceeds or is greater than the basic rights and freedoms of the individual. She believes that this is demonstrated by our acceptance of our medical socialist system. She believes that Canadians are willing to have less freedom and liberty than our American neighbours because we trust our Government more and are more willing to concede. Perhaps that is why she has never acknowledged the human and legal rights I have and feels comfortable hiding behind the Constitution and Charter of Rights and Freedoms.

How dare I contest what the State has proclaimed in Whiten v. Pilot Insurance Company SCC 27229 even though I was not on trial? No Canadian will ever accept the idea that the State has greater powers than individual citizens where their legal, moral and democratic rights have been violated by the state as in this case. Perhaps the CBC, CTV, Globe & Mail and Toronto Star should challenge her contention about our rights. If that is the case and we do lack the individual rights proclaimed in the Constitution of the United States, than we should elect a Government that will place citizen rights at least on par with that of the State. Who is out there defending Canadians? Why would the Prime Minister of Canada go to bat for the individual?

The definition of the word democracy contrasts with the speech of the Chief Justice that appears in Black's Law Dictionary. To quote, "Democracy is that form of government in which the sovereign power resides in and is exercised by the whole body of free citizens, as distinguished from a monarchy, aristocracy, or oligarchy. According to the theory of a pure democracy, every citizen should participate directly in the business of governing, and the legislative assembly should comprise the whole people." If this is not the definition of democracy in Canada according to the Supreme Court of Canada, then we fall short of the true meaning and intent of the word. Without adhering to the meaning of the word democracy, the Supreme Court or any Court in the Country is capable of depriving an individual of his or her rights with no recourse.

The Chief Justice is well aware that by her statement, she is empowering the state, which includes all levels of government; with greater powers than its individual citizens and that this is contrary to the ultimate definition of democracy. Therefore if she is not supporting democracy as defined then how can she define our society as being democratic? It either is or it isn't.

If the Chief Justice assessed the use of my name and the allegations made as to whether my democratic rights were denied by the Court, then she necessarily has to conclude that my democratic rights were denied and violated by the Supreme Court of Canada.

Clearly the Chief Justice would have a problem with a part of President Barack Obama's speech to the United Nations in his first term, when he quoted the former Unites States Attorney General, Robert F. Kennedy as follows: "As Robert Kennedy said, "the individual man, the child of God, is the touchstone of value, and all society, groups, the state, exist for his benefit."

CHAPTER SEVENTEEN

Universal Prescriptivism and Moral Indifference

One of the great philosophers of our time was a person by the name of R. M. Hare who attempted to provide an ethical theory for making morally correct judgments. The purpose of this article is not to provide a philosophical critique on the theory proposed by R. M. Hare but to understand how, using his understanding of moral theories, the Supreme Court of Canada, regarding the reasons for judgment, in Whiten v. Pilot Insurance Company, made the moral decision to name me as a form of punishment. What moral theory was Supreme Court Judge using when making the decision to name a person who had not given evidence had not testified and was described by those who did testify. Why was it necessary for me to be ambushed by this decision after the Supreme Court of Canada judgment was rendered and published to the public and around the world on the Internet?

There are two kinds of moral theories that guide the judgments of people when making decisions or in this case a ruling. The distinction is between descriptivist and non-descriptivist theories or prescriptivism. The first is based on a truth-condition theory and the second is based on what ought to be the case. The question remains whether the Supreme Court applied a moral principle of reasoning when naming me in the reasons for judgment or was the name included without a moral reason.

Does the Supreme Court of Canada follow a moral theory of reasoning when making judgments and is this moral theory based on descriptive or prescriptive theory or both? The prescriptive moral theory of R. M. Hare indicated that an 'ought'-statement maybe specific, detailed and complex. Clearly the Supreme Court of Canada did not explain the purpose for displaying my name or explain how this duty became a moral imperative that was not described in evidence and not described in previous judgments for this case before the Court of Appeal for Ontario and the Superior Court of Justice. Their reasons were not based on a descriptive account of evidence or precedence. Therefore the Supreme Court was using a form of prescriptive moral reasoning when making the decision to include my name in this judgment. The Supreme Court Judge attempts to describe my thoughts and my moral behaviour as if I ought not to have had those thoughts. He cannot describe the behaviour or any fact about me because there was no evidence about me in the case. However it became necessary to tie my name to the moral conclusions in this judgment because the Judge could not describe the person he was formulating a moral judgment about in his factual reasons for judgment.

The Supreme Court Judge stated as a fact that I ought not to have taken a position that would have influenced the Executives of Pilot Insurance Company to have a train of thought that contradicted what would otherwise have been a morally correct train of thought. Does the Judge formulate this fact because of evidence that describes the true or false characteristics of my actions? His only reference is to point to my name appearing, badly inscribed on the first page of a report. There is no factual evidence regarding any statements made by me or any other witness to support the Judge's facts about me. This Supreme Court Judge does not elucidate or provide any factual evidence for reference which would allow a truly objective thinker to understand how the use of my name is supported by facts. He points to a report to my attention and hopes that this alone will support an inference he has made about the causation between my name irrespective of the evidence given by the author of that letter, and Pilot Insurance Company regardless of the accuracy of the title used to identify me.

The Supreme Court Judge uses my name similar to the way an ostensive definition describes an indescribable object. He can only point to the name but does not describe his understanding of the individual or why he uses the name. He even misleads the reader by at first giving my name a significant management title. Only when he is caught by very person he is abusing, does he correct the title of my occupation. However the Judge makes this correction without explaining how a fact can be incorrect in both contexts and he does not provide a description of the role I had while I was an employee at Pilot Insurance Company. Most if not all employees in the free world understand the difference between management and employees or subordinates, but not this Judge who continues to describe me in his facts in this judgment as if I was still a manager in a role that would allow fiduciary responsibility.

If the Supreme Court of Canada was using a descriptivist moral philosophy when isolating and displaying the name Chris Porter as a moral imperative, then they should have provided examples of the deliverances of the wisdom that exemplify this precedence. Where in the Supreme Court of Canada rulings, have there ever been any precedents that would support their use my name? Is this an example of descriptivist moral reasoning? Clearly the only possible moral theory they can rely upon is a universal moral form of prescriptive theory.

In other words they assigned the word ought to their description of me. I ought not to have taken a position that the claim should be disputed. The Judge even says in his factual reasons that I ought not to have held that idea for a longer than an acceptable period of time. (What ever that is?). The Judge and the Supreme Court of Canada were not acting on a precedent case when they made a factual ruling in their judgment, that my name should be exemplified and ridiculed by society. Did they make their decision because of a prescriptivism moral theory that I ought not to have taken a position rather than pointing out a description of a violation of a rule or law?

This is how immoral decisions are made when the method of argument you have relied upon and which is the basis of the moral principles of law, are twisted to make a proposed illogical fact, factually sounding. If the Supreme Court of Canada were bound to follow a descriptivist theory for their deliverances to be correct, it does not make rational sense to suddenly introduce universal prescriptivism with the universality of 'ought'—propositions and other normative or evaluative statements about me when this is not based on facts and is unprecedented. Especially when precedent is how the Supreme Court of Canada, create law.

The problem with moral descriptivism as it is applied to rules and law, is that it uses truth as the basis for it's conclusions and truth is based on the theory that we can know that some moral judgments are true. These moral propositions are determined by precedent case law. The problem with the Judgment to include my name is that I did not have any status or a complete description of my evidence in this case and therefore the Supreme Court of Canada were not relying upon descriptive moral reasoning when exemplifying and using my name as a basis for the judgment.

This unprecedented act by the Supreme Court of Canada would only have helped those who wanted to deflect attention away from corporate responsible. In its findings, the Supreme Court of Canada must have been aware that the emphasis by Pilot of lower level employees was without precedence. There was even evidence which contradicted the way in which I was described in the Supreme Court of Canada reasons. This aspect of the reasons for judgment was unprecedented and wrong. Why is there not any avenue available to challenge the decision used to use my name? They cannot defend their own moral theory in what guided their reasons for using the reference to my name in the reasons for judgment. In their findings in reference to my name is not based on descriptivist or non-descriptivist, prescriptive moral theory.

Perhaps the Supreme Court of Canada broke its own procedure for arriving at a just and moral decision and may have in fact committed an immoral act. No matter which moral principle the Supreme Court of Canada followed, it must be universally applied and therefore if a person's name appears on correspondence and that correspondence is before the Supreme Court of Canada, that person's name should be used in the reasons for judgment regardless of that person's status as a witness and regardless of whether that person's rights under the law were considered. We should see a lot more instances of this type of naming by the Supreme Court of Canada in every future judgment, in order for their reasons to be morally correct in this incidence.

Some of the material above was described in a book by R.M. Hare entitled Freedom and Reason published by The Oxford Press 1963

The manuscript for this book was sent by email to the President of AVIVA a number of years ago. I asked him to provide me with his comments on the issues raised in the Supreme Court of Canada Ruling that were damaging my reputation.

I specifically asked him to address the conflicting testimony of the independent adjuster about the train of thought quoted by the Supreme Court of Canada in its ruling where the judgment initially describes me as the catalyst, in the denial of Whitens fire claim, not the management of Pilot Insurance Company who were only receiving material.

In response to my request, the President of AVIVA provides an email response described below, that does not address the first few paragraphs including paragraph 7 of the reasons for judgment where the Supreme Court of Canada uses my name in that passage and goes on to describe my title and role. He also does not address the implications of AVIVA being able to avoid the consequences of being identified as the 'Rogue' insurance company that methodically denied the claim of their insured with their employee being sacrificed, who was not middle management and was not in a position to settle or deny their claim.

In our email exchange he was defending the executives involved, the President and CEO of Pilot Insurance Company, Executive Vice President and Secretary of Pilot Insurance Company, the Assistant Vice President In Charge of Claims for Pilot Insurance Company and the Claims Manager for Pilot Insurance Company.

The President of AVIVA responded by basically trying to create the impression that the executives mentioned were only made known by the material on the file with which they were copied and therefore the misconduct was not restricted to lower employees including Chris Porter, which is the opposite of what happened and the then President of AVIVA was well aware of the facts.

We have investigated the situation per your request and we find no factual basis in support of your position and therefore we deny your allegations. In particular, with respect to what seems to be your main concern, we never have tried to portray you as the sole individual responsible for the "train of thought" or handling of the case. We, in fact, conceded the contrary in our factum and the Supreme Court Judge made specific reference to it. The Supreme Court Judge clearly states in paragraph 16 of the decision:

"in its factum before this Court, Pilot also conceded that in addition to the Senior Claims Examiner and the Branch Manager, the latter's superior, (BLANK) (assistant to the Vice-President in Charge of claims), [was] copied with all of the material on the file. The AVP reported to the (BLANK), Executive Vice President and Secretary". The misconduct was therefore not restricted to middle level management but was made known to the directing minds of the respondent company."

We are not prepared to get into a further debate on these matters with you given there is no factual basis for your allegations and the decision places responsibility on others as well as you. We consider this matter closed.

CHAPTER EIGHTEEN

Collateral Damage

My litigation libel actions with a Montreal law firm entailed a number of steps on my part. I ended up hiring three lawyers and having examinations for discoveries in Montreal, Quebec and Toronto, Ontario. The following is an account of the Court actions in Ontario before the case finally resolved. Unfortunately it had little effect since disclosure of the event was curtailed as a result of the agreement arranged by my final lawyer.

My lawyer, Christopher Ashby represented me in my libel actions as following;

Chris Porter v Robinson Sheppard Shapiro, to the Court of Appeal for Ontario, Docket: C42157, reversing 2004 June 29, Ontario Superior Court of Justice File No. 03-CV-243741 CM2 and before the Ontario Superior Court of Justice File No's.; 03-CV-243741, 04-CV-262007 CM2., resulting in a successful resolution of my libel action with Robinson Sheppard Shapiro and Mariella De Stefano.

DATE: 20050111
DOCKET: C42157

COURT OF APPEAL FOR ONTARIO

RE: CHRIS PORTER (Plaintiff/Appellant) v. ROBINSON SHEPPARD
           SHAPIRO AND MARIELLA DE STEFANO
           (Defendants/Respondents)

BEFORE: McMURTRY C.J.O., CATZMAN AND LANG JJ.A.

COUNSEL: Christopher Ashby
           for the appellant

           D. Bruce MacDougall
           for the respondents

HEARD &   January 11, 2005
ENDORSED:

On appeal from the order of Justice R. Pitt dated June 29, 2004.

APPEAL BOOK ENDORSEMENT

[1]   We are of the view that the words complained of by the appellant in both statements of claim are capable of a defamatory meaning and therefore the appellant is entitled to have a trial of that issue.

[2]   With respect to the defence of qualified privilege, we are of the opinion that the evidentiary basis before the motions judge was not sufficient to resolve that question at this early stage of the litigation.

[3]   The appeal is therefore allowed and the decision of the motions judge is set aside. The appellant is entitled to his costs before the motions judge fixed in the amount of $6,792.97 and of the appeal in the amount of $4,727.06.

"the above quote from the Court of Appeal for Ontario is a replica and not represented as an official version of the judgment"

Even after finally establishing my role as an examiner at Pilot Insurance Company before the Ontario Superior Court, the Chief Justice of the Supreme Court of Canada, refused to acknowledge the truth of my involvement and allow my lawyer to present my case to the Supreme Court of Canada.

I continue to hope for the day when the Supreme Court of Canada acknowledges the truth and corrects the record.

I would further like to acknowledge with thanks to both

Mr. Roger McConchie and Mr. Brock Ketchum for revealing to the public the truth.

Business Edge Archives » Brock Ketcham
Insurance lawsuits a bruising experience

Company has 'taken lessons seriously'

By Brock Ketcham—For Business Edge
Published: 08/03/2006—Vol. 3, No. 16

One person's unremitting nightmare can, for another, be the stuff of humdrum life at the office.

Take lawsuits, for example. A fire destroys a business; the owner files an insurance claim. The insurer denies the claim with an arson defence, leaving the claimant with no choice but to sue or abandon the claim.

Former Pilot Insurance Co. employee Chris Porter of Toronto has navigated the litigation process both as an insurance employee and as a private individual.

Having recently emerged successfully from private litigation in which he battled Canada's legal system in a matter he says deprived him—at least temporarily—of his professional reputation, he sums up the experience thus: "It took an incredible toll."

Porter, a senior claims examiner, was involved in the initial handing of a 1994 Ontario fire claim that led to the landmark February 2002 Supreme Court of Canada judgment in Whiten vs Pilot Insurance Co.

The judgment restored a 1996 jury award of $1 million in punitive damages, a rarely employed sanction.

Homeowner Daphne Whiten and her husband Keith (who died a couple of years ago from cancer) had Pilot Insurance as their insurer when—on a bitterly cold winter's night—a fire believed to have been ignited by a faulty heater destroyed their rural home near Haliburton, Ont.

The Ontario insurer, the Supreme Court noted, used an arson defence to avoid paying the claim. But the Whitens, despite being in desperate financial circumstances, managed to claw their way up to the Supreme Court through the gritty hard work of Bay Street lawyer Gary Will.

The outcome proved costly for an industry that, in Canada, had hitherto been dealt with leniently by the courts in cases where bad faith was proven. The previous largest punitive damages ever awarded against an insurer in Canada was $15,000.

With the maximum suddenly having been increased, Canada's insurers now found themselves in unfamiliar legal territory—one that resembled the habitat of their American brethren that can be financially punishing to those who abuse the economic superiority they hold over most of their clients.

The fallout from this profoundly significant case has continued in the years since the Supreme Court decision. Chris Porter, who ended up as collateral damage in this sordid affair, has only just recently begun rebuilding his reputation after leaving Pilot in April 2000.

Porter fought hard, taking on the judicial, insurance and legal establishment in a grim quest to set the record straight about who was really responsible for the decision to stonewall the Whiten claim.

The original decision, which the trial judge noted was abetted by an external lawyer acting in the handling of the claim, was made at Pilot's executive level.

However, the Supreme Court's Whiten vs Pilot Insurance judgment instead made it look like Porter played a significant role. Porter was cast as a management-level decision-maker, drawing attention away from the higher-ups who were actually responsible.

In March 2002, legal counsel acting for Porter wrote the Supreme Court about the error. Porter's correct title was "senior claims examiner," the lawyer wrote; not "senior claims manager" as stated in the judgment.

The court issued a revised judgment in April 2002 that corrected Porter's title.

But Porter protested this didn't go far enough. He wanted the judgment to include information about his handling of the claim, such as his desire to settle for an amount that would have covered the loss. "My role was completely opposite to what was described in the reasons for judgment," he wrote the court.

The court wrote back that this information was not put before the lower court, so there was nothing further it could do.

Later, Porter sued Montreal law firm Robinson Sheppard Shapiro for defamation over its publication on its website of the erroneous material from the Supreme Court's initial lawsuit, hard copies of which it sent to 450 of its clients (many of whom are insurance companies).

Extensive litigation ensued, with Porter winning the right to a trial after appealing a summary judgment dismissing his lawsuit. On the third day of the trial in January 2006, Robinson Sheppard Shapiro settled the lawsuit by acknowledging that Porter did not deny the Whiten claim.

Sally Turney, vice-president of corporate communications with Pilot's new parent company Aviva Canada Inc. in Toronto, declined comment. She explained that Pilot does not comment on matters involving past or current employees.

Stuart Kistruck, a Pilot president and CEO who left the position following a high-level shakeup in 2003, told me in November 2002 when I was researching another article that his company regretted how the claim was handled.

"This is one of those cases that got off the rails," Kistruck said. "I'd like to give the Pilot side of the story. But there is not a Pilot side of the story . . . I wish this never happened."

James Hewitt, Kistruck's successor, says the Whiten affair was an isolated case.

"We have taken the lessons that we learned from this experience seriously," wrote the recently retired Hewitt. "We have made changes to our claims policies and procedures to ensure that situations like this are handled differently."

Insurance Bureau of Canada spokesman John Karapita of Toronto said the Porter affair was not considered "an industry issue," therefore the IBC is not involved.

Porter's insurance background proved to be a crucial asset in addressing the difficult challenges he faced in repairing the damage to his name.

Over the years, I've met businesspeople who have been wronged by insurers or lawyers and then destroyed by an obsessive, ineffectual quest for justice doomed at the outset by a lack of the prerequisite financial, emotional and intellectual resources.

It was interesting, therefore, to observe Porter experiencing how, for ordinary mortals, a lawsuit becomes an all-consuming enterprise. As a private individual in a position adverse to that of a powerful industry, he even had difficulty finding a lawyer willing to bring his case to court. "I was like a leper," he says.

The legal ordeal wiped out Porter's life savings. Though he was able to find similar-paying work with another insurer in Toronto after leaving Pilot, the income was not enough to cover his legal costs.

"I know now what poor Keith and Daphne (Whiten) went through," he says.

When the other insurance company he was working for let him go the year the Supreme Court handed down its decision.

The IBC's Karapita was nonplussed over this assertion. "From our perspective, this is about an individual that I've never heard of."